REVOLUTION PRICING

# PRICE FOR GROWTH

## CONDENSED AND ABRIDGED

A Revolutionary Step-by-Step Approach
To Massively Increase the Value of Your Company
By Leveraging Focused Pricing Strategies

JEFF ROBINSON

Published by:
Revolution Pricing LLC, Houston, TX
RevolutionPricing.com



For additional information related to this book, please visit the book's website at:

PriceForGrowth.com

ISBN: 978-1-7368225-3-1

Credits
Cover Design: Pankaj Vishwakarma
Original Editing: J.D. Ho
Print Design: Bhagchand

To my wife and best friend, Michelle.

Thank you for believing in me and standing by me through all the good times and the bad times. You've given me more than you will ever know.

And to my three wonderful daughters: Whitney, Jessie, and Sydney.

You've given me the privilege of seeing the world through younger eyes, and you've always encouraged me to look out for the underdogs.

And to my mother, Kathy Robinson.

You've always been my biggest cheerleader. Even when I thought I was pretty average, you thought I was great.

And to my large extended family.

You've always been a great support net throughout my whole life.

# Contents

Introduction ..... 1

**Part 1: Foundations**

Chapter 1: Redefining the Pricing Journey ..... 5

Chapter 2: A Tale of Two Companies (Case Parable 1) ..... 11

Chapter 3: The Growth Mindset and Pricing ..... 19

Chapter 4: The Five Sacred Metrics of Pricing Success ..... 25

Chapter 5: The Story of Leroy Studemont (Case Parable 2) ..... 31

**Part 2: Customer Relationships**

Chapter 6: Losing the Pricing Tug-o-War ..... 41

Chapter 7: The Importance of Trustworthy Prices ..... 49

Chapter 8: Sara's Pricing Overhaul (Case Parable 3) ..... 55

Chapter 9: The Age of Millennials ..... 63

Chapter 10: Your Key Customer Categories ..... 67

Chapter 11: Hypothesis-Based Pricing Transformation (Case Parable 4) ..... 77

**Part 3: Building Focused Pricing Strategies**

Chapter 12: The Concept of Elasticity vs. Growth ..... 85

Chapter 13: Objective-Driven Pricing Strategies ..... 91

Chapter 14: Applying the 80/20 Principle ..... 101

Chapter 15: Pricing Strategies to Increase Customer Acquisition ..... 107

Chapter 16: Pricing Strategies to Incrase Existing Customer Revenues ..... 115

Chapter 17: Pricing Strategies to Reduce Customer Churn ..... 121

Chapter 18: Pricing Strategies to Expand Margins ..... 127

Chapter 19: Pricing Strategies to Reduce Risk ..... 133

**Part 4: Putting It All Together**

Chapter 20: The Complete Step-by-Step Process ..... 139

Chapter 21: TransformaCo's Step-By-Step Journey (Case Parable 5) ..... 147

Chapter 22: Moving Forward and Taking Action ..... 153

# Acknowledgements

So many people deserve to be acknowledged for helping me get here.

First of all, I'd like to acknowledge some of the key thought leaders, some of whom are referred to as the "Godfathers of Pricing" in the relatively small community of pricing experts and practitioners. But I learned and benefited tremendously from the discussions and writings of Dan Nimer, Tom Nagle, Reed Holden, Mike Marn, Herman Simon, and Craig Zawada.

I'd also like to recognize Eric Mitchell, the founder of The Professional Pricing Society, which is currently the largest professional organization for pricing on the planet. Today, his son Kevin is leading what his father started, advance pricing knowledge and expertise around the globe.

I must also acknowledge several other key individuals who spent years with me working through ideas and putting them into practice to challenge them and perfect them, including (in alphabetical order): Gary Alexander, Navin Aswal, Rohan Bairat, Neil Biehn, Erik Bleyl, Steve Bondi, Andy Boyd, Christine Byun, Rob Christenson, Roxy Cramer, Ajay Damani, Jacqui Davis, Michael Davis, Bhavit Desai, Bill Dudziak, Sean Ferguson, Doug Fuehne, Steve Goldstein, Ed Gonzalez, Tom Gorin, MG Gurbaxani, Chuck Hinkle, Phil Holladay, Anshu Jalora, Sunil John, Matt Johnson, Royce Kallesen, Vernon Lennon, Stephan Liozu, Ashish Malhotra, Augustin Manchon, Kevin McCraw, Oscar Moreno, Joanna Papakonstantinou, Todd Pate, Harold Peck, Adriana Rapolla, Wilbur Reid, Rob Reiner, Tony Ruggiero, John Salch, Patrick Scheidau, Walt Sepaniac, Justin Silver, Martin Simoncic, Alex Smith, Mark Stevens, Charles Sweeney, Ted Valkov, Ulrich von Beck, Geoff Webb, David White, Steve Wilkins, Wagner Williiams, and many others I don't have room to name individually..

I would like to thank key people who gave me opportunities to grow my career and expand my skill set under their leadership, including Ivan Boyd, Mark Lamp, Greg Smith, Bert Winemiller, Charlie Murphy, Ron Woestemeyer, Andres Reiner, Tom Dziersk, and Erik Bleyl.

And to many others I haven't named who have helped me along the way, I say Thank You!

# About the Author

Jeff Robinson has spent over 20 years of his career designing, marketing, selling, implementing, and consulting in the field of pricing. He has worked with over 100 companies across 15 different industries to help them solve their highest priority pricing challenges. He has authored several blogs, articles, white papers, presentations, and training materials, and he has presented at pricing and industry conferences on the subject of pricing and pricing strategy. He has held several executive leadership positions, leading product management, data science and innovation, consulting services, business development, and sales and marketing. His real-world experience is built on the foundation of a strong education with a bachelor's degree in Economics from Brigham Young University and an MBA from Rice University.

His current LinkedIn profile can be found at:

https://www.linkedin.com/in/jeffrobinson4/

And his Author website can be found at:

https://jeffrobinson.com/

# Introduction

Since the release of ***Price for Growth***, many people have communicated to me that they wish there were a "Cliff Notes" style summary of this book, so they could digest the content without devoting several hours to consume a 337-page book.

I was initially reluctant to create a condensed and abridged version because I felt like the concepts were too important to gloss over without getting into the detail. But after further consideration, I felt like I could put together meaningful summaries of each chapter that hit the high points, based on what I felt was most important, and still allow the reader to refer back to the full version to answer anything that wasn't intuitively obvious.

The result is this condensed and abridged version, which reduces the main content detail by approximately 75% while leaving the full chapter summaries at the end of each chapter roughly the same as the complete book. This version contains one-third the amount of words as the full version to allow for a much faster read for first time readers and a more succinct review for those who have already consumed the full version.

I hope you enjoy this condensed version, and now I will jump into the condensed version of the original introduction below…

**Abbreviated Version of the Original Introduction**

What if you could double the value of your company in less than a year just by using the right focused pricing strategy?

What if we've been wrong about profit-focused pricing strategies? What if our efforts to grow margins were actually hurting our ability to maximize long-term profit growth? **What if we've been missing out on the most powerful ways to use pricing to maximize the value of the company?**

For the last two decades, companies have been told that a 1% increase in price will, on average, translate to an 11% increase in profits. During that time, an entire pricing solution industry has exploded, fueled by the quest to help companies achieve that extra 1%, in hopes of achieving that extra profit that's been "left on the table."

Many of the short-term results have shown promise. A multitude of companies have invested millions of dollars in pricing solutions, and many of them have reported price improvements as high as 2%–3% or more, easily exceeding the quest for the extra 1%. Unfortunately, these reported benefits are seldom able to continue for more than two to three years.

The reality is most companies are using the wrong pricing strategies—pricing for margin when they really want to be growing—and missing out on the most impactful opportunities to grow the value of their companies.

That's why, after two decades of designing, building, selling, and implementing pricing solutions (that have now reached hundreds of companies whose revenues total over $1 trillion), I developed the **five sacred metrics of pricing success** and a comprehensive framework for identifying impact and deploying pricing strategies to have maximum impact on company value.

This is something that many companies are missing. While most people have all the basic bits of knowledge necessary for creating successful pricing strategies, what's missing is a framework to bring all this knowledge into a cohesive structure for making decisions. That's what I'm giving you in this book—a revolutionary, step-by-step approach to create the best pricing strategies to maximize the value of your company.

If you are a CFO, CEO, COO, VP of Pricing, VP of Growth, VP of Sales, or any manager or executive who has responsibility for company growth and/or pricing, this book is for you.

Reading and understanding what is in these pages will help you ensure that your pricing strategies are working for you and not against you. The stakes are too high, and the knowledge in this book is too valuable to ignore.

This condensed and abridged summary of ***Price for Growth: A Revolutionary Step-by-Step Approach to Massively Increase the Value of Your Company by Leveraging Focused Pricing Strategies*** will allow you to get the main points of the full 337-page book in one-third the time. For each chapter of the book, I provide a condensed chapter overview followed by the actual chapter summary found at the end of each chapter in the complete full edition of the book.

I hope you enjoy the abbreviated trip!

PART 1

# Foundations

*One must have first of all a solid foundation*

—Sri Aurobindo

CHAPTER 1

# Redefining the Pricing Journey

*Every product and service sold since the beginning of time has had a price assigned to it. Setting that price is among the most crucial, most profit-sensitive decisions that companies make. Ironically, very few companies price well.*

—*The Price Advantage* © 2004, Marn, Roegner, Zawada

## Chapter Overview

As one might expect, the pricing solution industry has exploded over the last twenty years. Today there are large and small software companies devoted to pricing. There are literally hundreds of consulting firms that collectively employ thousands of consultants focused on improving pricing across many of the world's most forward-thinking companies. Several thought-provoking books have been written by a variety of authors on the topic of pricing, each adding to the collective knowledge of pricing best practices. For ages, companies have been building their own custom pricing solutions, and this practice has only accelerated over the last few years. For better or for worse, the business world has been flooded with pricing solutions.

But, for the most part, the billions of dollars invested in pricing software and consulting solutions over the years have not produced the sustained profit growth that was promised or expected. Many companies are still looking for that silver bullet solution that will finally deliver results in a sustainable fashion, year after year.

Pricing opportunities have not gone away. Pricing still has considerable leverage on profitability, probably more than any other single variable, and yet it remains one of the last frontiers still left unconquered.

**Why are the majority of today's pricing solutions failing to deliver long-term, sustainable profit growth?** In short, the answer is because most solutions focus on only one aspect of pricing (typically margin improvement), where a one-time correction may be needed. And once that correction is achieved, further corrective effort does not lead to improvement. As my good friend Harold Peck once said many years ago, "Raising prices is not a sustainable source of profit growth."

But companies want to see rapid return on their investments, and the easiest way to show rapid returns is to implement select price increases to show increased margins. The problem is that it's not usually possible to continue to grow margins every year over a sustained period of time.

Without a comprehensive framework that ties pricing actions to the metrics that drive real growth in all present and future profits (including customer acquisition, growth, and retention), pricing solutions will lose their potency as their targeted corrective actions stall out. Most pricing solutions based on selectively raising prices for expanded margins tend to ignore these other critical customer relationship metrics and the risks imposed upon them when prices are increased.

The framework I will share with you brings pricing objectives and business objectives together through a collection of **five "sacred" metrics**. These metrics will bring clarity to the size and impact of opportunities and how they translate to the growth of the value of your company, not just for the short term, but for the long term. And you will be able to see the connection between today's pricing decisions and all future profit flows.

One of the things that absolutely baffles me is why high-growth-aspiring companies prefer to act like profit-harvesting companies in how they approach their own pricing strategies.

The famous Boston Consulting Group (BCG) company classification model describes four different types of companies, as follows:

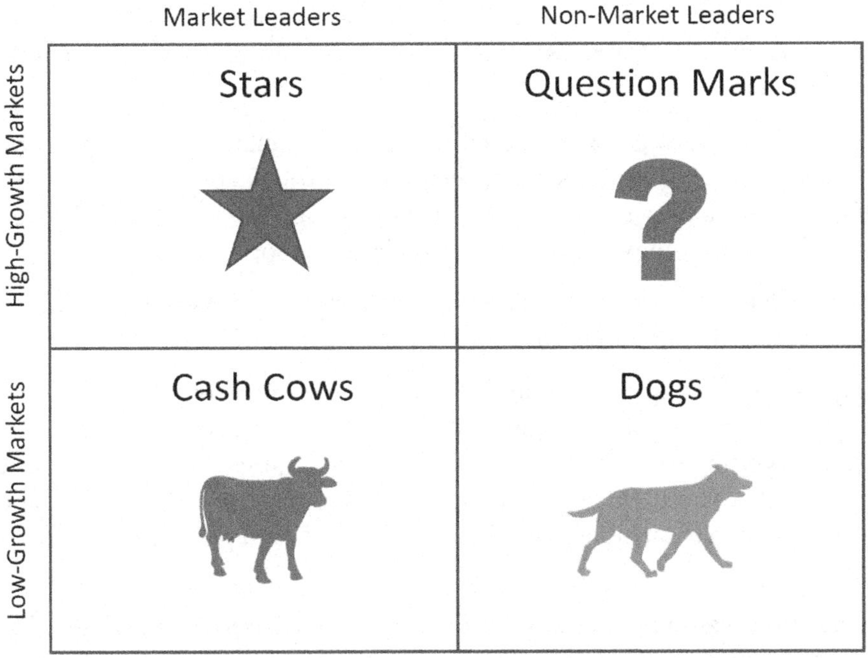


- **Stars**: market leaders in high-growth markets
- **Cash Cows**: market leaders in low-growth markets
- **Question Marks**: non-market-leaders in high-growth markets
- **Dogs**: non-market-leaders in low-growth markets

From a growth strategy perspective, **Stars** and **Question Marks** should theoretically focus on growth, either to protect their own market leadership as Stars, or to attempt to overtake Stars. Not focusing on growth could lead to a massive, missed opportunity to either become a Star or stay a Star. In high-growth markets, winners are determined based on who wins the market-share battle.

Conversely, Cash Cows and Dogs have little opportunity for growth because they are in low-growth markets, and they're more likely to be focused on harvesting profits.

How would you classify your company? Are you a **Star**? Are you a **Question Mark**? If so, it only makes sense to be focused on growth strategies.

There is a significant difference between **growth pricing strategies** and **profit-harvesting pricing strategies**. In profit harvesting, the objective metric is typically profit margin percentage. Growth pricing strategies focus on the objective metrics of revenues, customers, and sales growth. Growth pricing strategies tend to focus on incentivizing the acceleration of customer acquisition, expanding revenues per customer, and reducing customer churn. And, in fact, growth strategies can often be harmed by attempting to increase profit margins.

I have seen too many growth-focused companies erroneously focus their pricing efforts on expanding margins, while their competitors focus on gobbling up market share. Chasing profits when you are fighting a market share battle is a fool's errand. You can pocket dividends, but at what cost?

Unfortunately, the cost may be a long-term leadership position that could otherwise have lasted for decades.

Today we are at a tipping point in the evolution of commerce; the old approaches to pricing simply won't be effective anymore. Not only are customers getting smarter, but their values are changing. Companies must adapt to succeed. Successful pricing strategies need to reflect a practical understanding of customer behavior, along with the needs, desires, and priorities that drive that behavior.

The most successful pricing strategies are ultimately based on what's good for the customer. Businesses live or die based on their ability to successfully attract customers and fill their needs. Good pricing practices keep profitable customers coming back year after year. This means you will need pricing metrics that look far beyond the present transaction opportunity in order to measure how well pricing helps to increase and sustain customer loyalty.

The world is moving quickly to e-commerce, and negotiated pricing is going away. Millennials are quickly becoming the dominant generation in charge of the majority of all purchase decisions, and Generation Z is right behind them. These new generations of customers will not accept the old ways of doing business because they have more choices than any previous generation. The chapters that follow provide the conceptual framework for how companies must price in the new reality of digital commerce in order to attract and grow the customer relationships that will power the growing streams of future profits.

## Chapter Summary

Despite the explosive growth of the pricing solutions industry, many companies are still struggling to find ways to use pricing to drive sustainable profit growth. Most margin-based pricing solutions lose momentum after achieving one or two years of successful results. Understanding why this happens is critical to charting a better path forward.

Growth-focused pricing strategies and profit-focused pricing strategies are both different and largely incompatible at their respective foundations. Most companies are growth-focused vs. profit-focused in the context of the famous BCG company classification model. Yet many of these growth-focused companies choose, for some reason, to implement profit-focused pricing strategies instead of growth-focused pricing strategies. This is a major problem which produces a logical inconsistency and a no-win situation. In order to be successful, growth companies need to implement growth-based pricing strategies.

Growth-based pricing strategies focus on new customer acquisition, existing customer retention, and existing customer revenue growth in order to drive sustainable, long-term profit growth, which ultimately drives up the value of the company. This means customer relationships matter more. At the same time, customer needs, attitudes, and behaviors are changing as the world evolves to digital commerce and as Millennials become the dominant generation of buyers. Customer buying experience is becoming more important than ever before, and this has major implications for how companies make and communicate pricing decisions.

This book offers a new and revolutionary approach to pricing which will help companies drive more sustainable profit growth, addressing both the challenges of the past and the challenges of today's evolving digital-enabled customers. The concepts and ideas in this book are certain to transform the way you think about pricing in the context of maximizing the value of your company. In the end, the purpose of this book is to show you how to make a dramatic impact on the value of your company by altering the ways you make pricing decisions, starting with the metrics you should use to prioritize potential pricing actions.

CHAPTER 2

# The Tale of Two Companies

**Case Parable 1: CommonCo Vs. GrowthCo**

## Chapter Overview

This chapter contains a "case parable" about two similar CFOs of two nearly identical companies, both of which manufacture and distribute synthetic leather gloves: Joe Durban, CFO of CommonCo, and Mary Matos, CFO of GrwothCo. Despite their similarities, they had very different strategies for growing profits. Joe's strategy was to try to keep pushing up margins, claiming they had a premium product which deserved progressively higher premium prices. Mary's strategy was focused on maintaining high levels of customer retention and new customer acquisition, essentially trying to grow profits through faster revenue growth vs. raising prices.

Over a 5-year period, Joe's strategy led to a 91% increase in profits, which was obtained by a 50% increase in gross margins percentage and 5% annual net revenue growth, which compounded to 27% over the five years. Because investors valued the company at a 5X profit multiple, his pricing strategy resulted in the value of the company increasing by 91%, from $31.3 million to $60 million. And his 10% stake grew by $2.9 million.

The following charts illustrate Joe's results:

**CommonCo Total Sales**
in $ millions

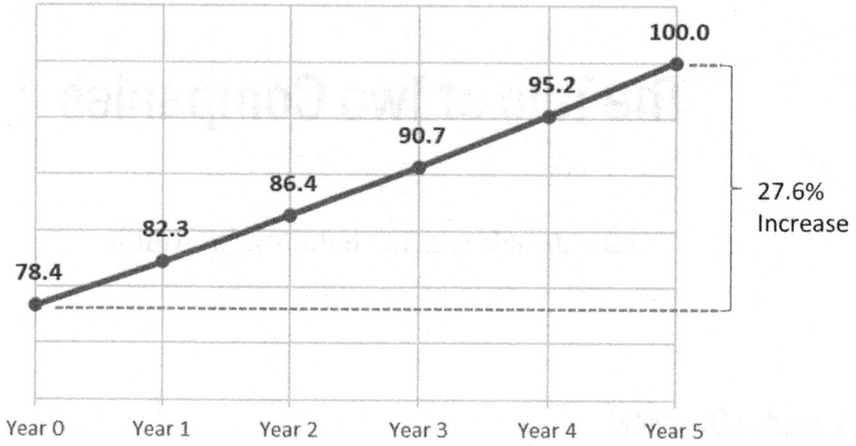


**CommonCo Total Profits**
in $ millions

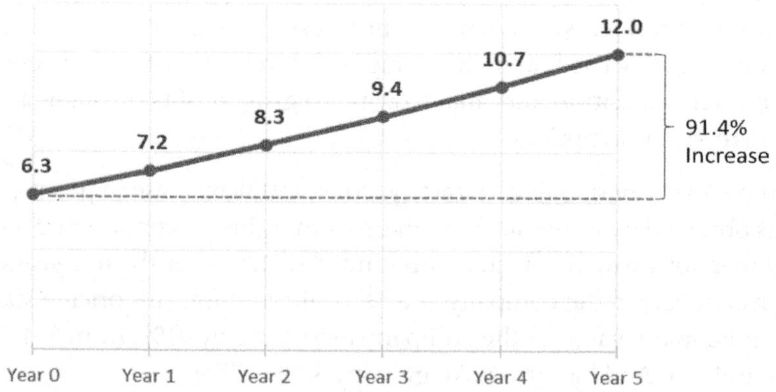

**CommonCo Total Company Value**
in $ millions

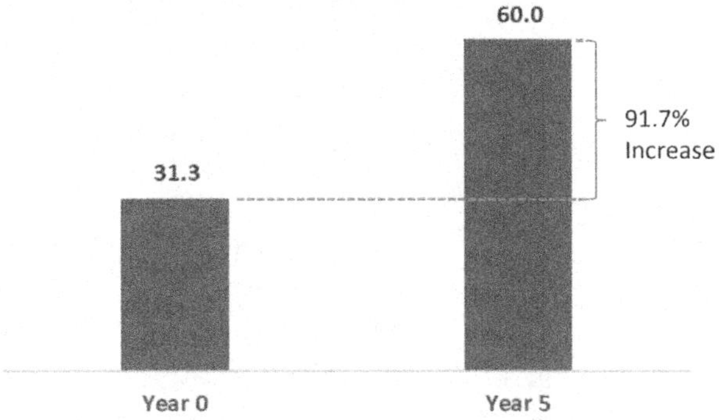


Even though Joe's metrics looked good on the surface, he worried a little about the fact that his 5% net growth rate was made up of a **new customer revenue acquisition rate** of 20% per year, offset against a **customer revenue churn rate** of 15%. CommonCo was losing approximately 15% of its customers every single year, which was higher than the average for the industry. But this was not really visible because most people just saw the net growth rate of 5% per year.

Conversely, Mary's strategy resulted in no real change in prices over the five years, but GrowthCo was able to achieve a net revenue growth rate of 18% per year by keeping her churn rate down to only 8% and her new customer acquisition rate around 26%. This 18% net growth rate compounded to almost 129% over the 5 years. And with no change in unit margins her total profits also grew by nearly 129%. And because her growth rate was so much higher, investors came to value her company by using a 10X profit multiple, which resulted in a company valuation of $143 million, an increase of $112 million over the 5 years. And her personal equity stake of 10% grew by $11.2 million.

The following charts illustrate Mary's performance:

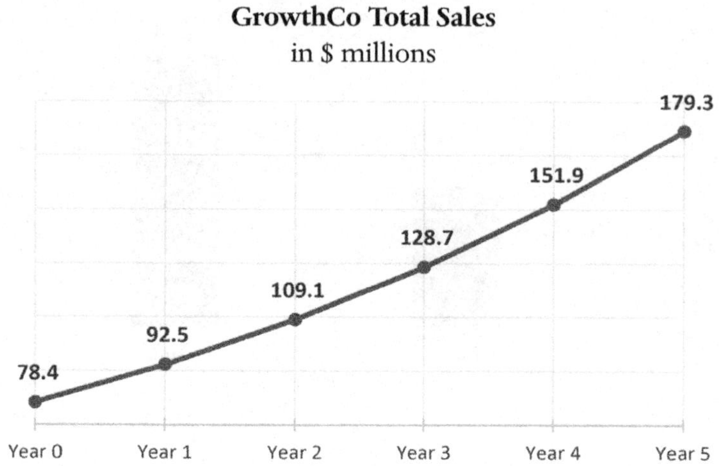


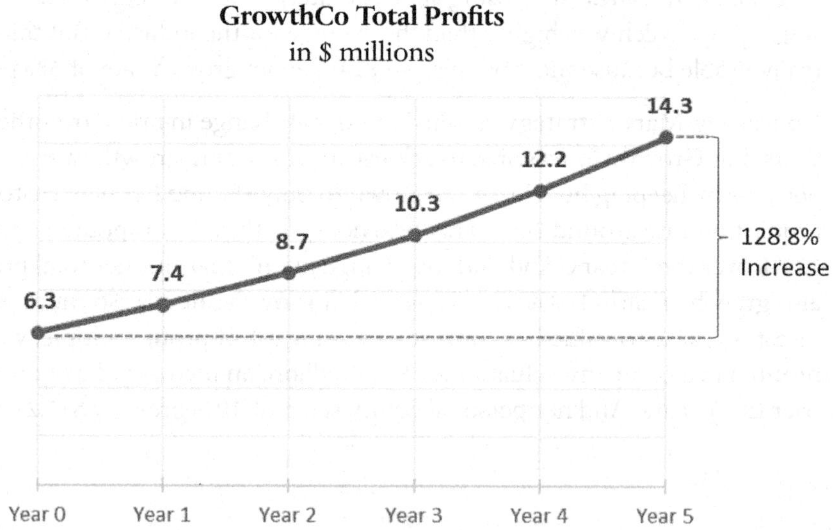

## Comparing the Two Companies

Somewhat ironically, GrowthCo's per-unit profit margins never exceeded 8%, but their total profits were now 19.5% higher than CommonCo's, despite the fact that CommonCo had driven per-unit profit margins up to 12%, as shown in the comparison chart below:

**Total Profits: CommonCo vs. GrowthCo**
in $ millions

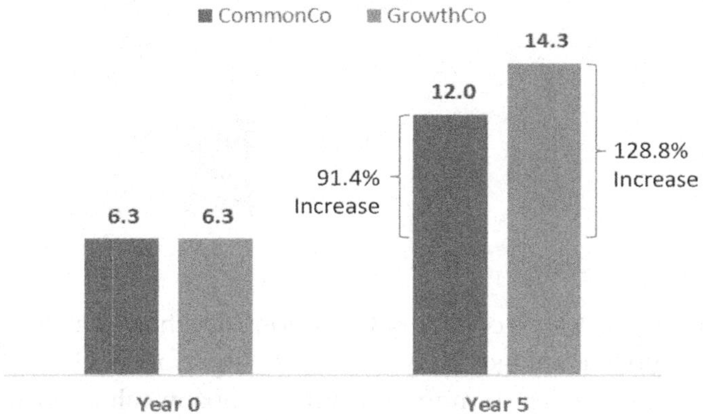


In fact, GrowthCo outperformed CommonCo on almost every metric except net profit margin percentage. After five years, GrowthCo's revenues had increased by 128.8% to $179.3M, as shown in the chart below:

**Total Sales: CommonCo vs. GrowthCo**
in $ millions

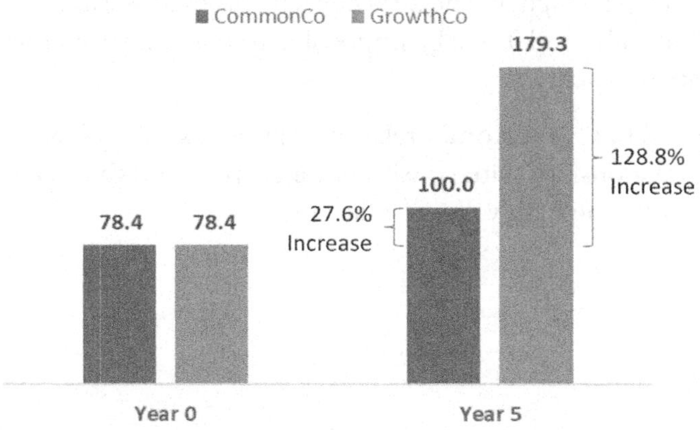

A comparison of company valuation growth is shown in the chart below:

**Total Company Valuation: CommonCo vs. GrowthCo**
in $ millions

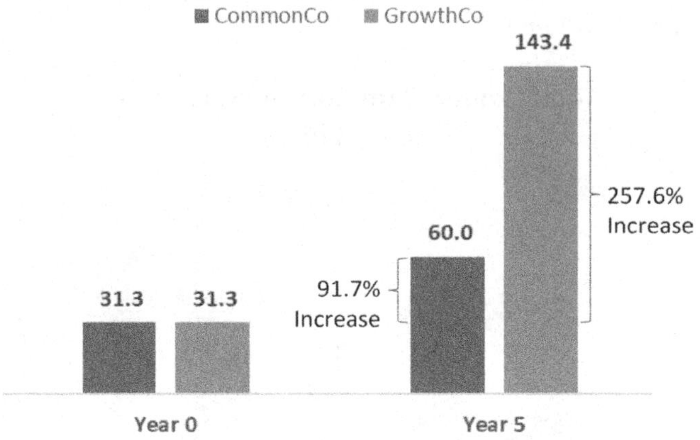


Despite the fact that Joe's company, CommonCo, achieved a 50% improvement in profit-margin percentage, Mary massively outperformed Joe from a total profit perspective, and even more so from a company valuation and personal wealth perspective.

But what's worse is that Joe's strategy elevated CommonCo's profit risk substantially. Joe's strategy of raising prices is not sustainable. By driving prices up every year, Joe was making CommonCo's customers pay significantly higher prices than his competitors' customers. And price is starting to become an issue for both new and existing customers. It is becoming less likely that customers will tolerate any further price increases. His already high churn rate will likely get even higher. The 20% new customer acquisition rate is likely drop dramatically. And it will be impossible to maintain even the relatively low growth rate of 5%.

While Joe has put his customer relationships at risk, Mary has strengthened her customer relationships with consistency and trust, and she has delivered on her strategy of offering high value at a fair price.

## Chapter Summary

The case parable comparison of CommonCo and GrowthCo illustrates many points that reinforce why growth-focused pricing strategies will almost always outperform margin-based pricing strategies, especially for growth-focused companies:

- Even though a company may appear to be doing well, in terms of both revenue growth and profitability, it is possible that it could be doing even better by changing elements of its pricing strategies.
- A myopic focus on profitability and margins can lead to suboptimal results if your main objective is to grow the value of the company.
- Just because it may be common practice to use a profit multiple to value a business doesn't mean growth doesn't matter. Investors will often pay a higher multiple for companies who have better growth. Growth rates always matter.
- Sometimes a company's growth is limited by churn—the loss of revenues from customers who are leaving. CommonCo's sales team was acquiring new customers at an annual rate of 20% of revenues. But because of the 15% churn, their net growth rate was much lower—only 5%.
- Continuously raising prices can add excessive risk to customer relationships and increase the probability of customer churn.

The future of pricing will be to focus on the growth and strength of customer relationships and to make efforts to reduce preventable churn.

CHAPTER 3

# The Growth Mindset and Pricing

*The reasonable man adapts himself to the world; the unreasonable one persists in trying to adapt the world to himself. Therefore, all progress depends on the unreasonable man.*

—George Bernard Shaw

## Chapter Overview

The way the pricing profession has evolved, it now carries mutually conflicting objectives. On one hand, Pricing is the champion of profit margins, measured by how much they are able to increase prices and margins over time. On the other hand, most pricing professionals instinctively understand that sales growth is critical for the company to maximize its value to shareholders. The conflict arises because experienced pricing people understand that raising prices and growing margins are ultimately in conflict with the objective of increasing sales and retaining customers. They are fundamentally different objectives that require fundamentally different strategies.

This inverse relationship between pricing and sales success can result in unnecessary psychological pressures. Because it is almost impossible to continuously raise prices and margins, pricing people often find themselves trying to rationalize why they actually do add value. This is a classic no-win situation, which can amplify feelings of insignificance, futility, and even depression. It can make normal people feel small and insignificant.

## The Scarcity Mindset

The scarcity mindset can be very demotivational. It can channel thoughts in a negative direction and impede a person's cognitive abilities. Psychologists have concluded that the lack or "scarcity" of something a person needs, whether physical or emotional, can cause the human brain to become overwhelmed and start to malfunction, sometimes in a way that can lead to counterproductive decisions that actually make the situation significantly worse. The symptoms of the scarcity mindset highlight a pattern of thinking that is more inwardly focused on protection rather than outwardly focused on opportunity.

The scarcity mindset can make things worse because it allows thinking to be dominated by problems and restrictions rather than opportunities and possibilities. It can lead to chronic stress that can reduce your mental and cognitive performance over time.

## The Growth Mindset

Whether you call it the "Growth Mindset," the "Abundance Mindset," or the "Expansive Mindset," it all leads to the same destination—the intellectual and psychological freedom to think in a world of infinite possibilities.

The key quality I've seen in the truly successful people I've ever met is that they convey a growth mindset. As a result, they are able to do more to make a bigger difference. They carry a happy, positive attitude, and they inspire others.

Transforming to a **growth mindset** is actually easy and self-reinforcing. Once you start to change how you think, you will find that it's easier to think that way all the time.

Start with a belief that success is possible; this will motivate you to look for pathways to succeed instead of giving up because a problem seems too difficult.

Shift to a belief that opportunities are everywhere, and there are multiple solutions to every problem. Remind yourself that you can always shift what isn't working.

Make it a priority to learn from every experience. Set aside time every day to learn. Read. Listen to audiobooks. Watch educational YouTube videos. Just learning and getting smarter will change your outlook. Learning will help you be resilient and look at setbacks as opportunities that will ultimately lead you to success. Being open to ideas and opinions from others opens new learning channels.

## Applying the Growth Mindset to Pricing

Start by imagining all the ways you can help your company grow. Don't limit this exploration to just pricing-related ideas. Write down your ideas, and share them with an intent to learn, grow, and improve.

Think about pricing actions that would help you and your company learn—about your customers, your products, your sales and marketing capabilities, your competitors, and yourself. Sometimes just thinking about potential actions will give you the needed perspective to arrive at the best solution.

Ask questions. Stimulate conversations.

Think outside the box. What are the "crazy" ideas you have about pricing? About value? About how to improve the lives of your customers? Let your crazy ideas spark discussions that might generate more ideas. Imagine how you might paint a picture of the opportunities in pricing to serve as a backdrop for a discussion with other executives. Pictures can trigger new ideas and thinking. Pictures are powerful ways to communicate. Here's an example that I've used before:

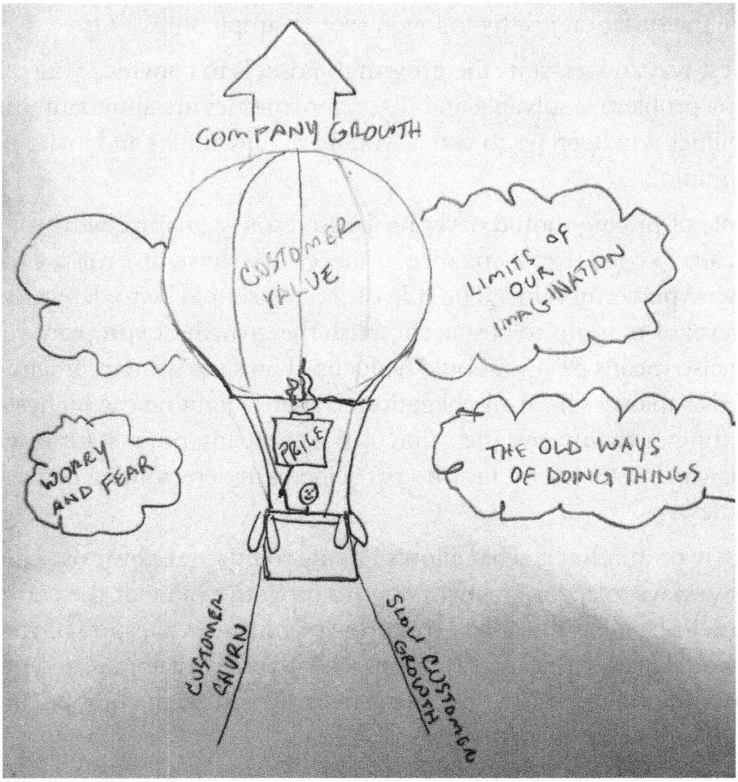

Communicate with others as a way to help them generate their own ideas. Help others understand what you understand. Use your knowledge of pricing to help others see opportunities that aren't otherwise easy to see.

## Chapter Summary

In this chapter, we've focused on the importance of having the right mindset in any role with pricing responsibility, highlighting some important ideas:

- In pricing roles, it can be easy to feel limited because of the inherent conflict between margin expansion and sales growth. It's important to be aware of this, so you can take appropriate actions to prevent falling into a scarcity mindset.
- The scarcity mindset occurs because a person feels a lack of something important in their life. If you let it stay, it can negatively affect your ability to think and make decisions, thereby preventing you from reaching your goals.
- The symptoms of the scarcity mindset include inward focus, fear of competition, fear of failure, and reluctance to change. If you detect these symptoms in either your life or the life of a team member, you can easily change the situation just by following some simple steps.
- The best way to kick-start the growth mindset is to convince yourself that any problem is solvable and that opportunities are abundant. Infinite possibilities will open up to you as you learn new things and invite new ways of thinking.
- The role of pricing should never be focused solely on improving margins. This leads to cognitive dissonance, unnecessary stress, and misuse of your otherwise powerful mind. The role of pricing should be to determine the right level of margins to best accomplish the growth of company value, which also means pricing should be focused on sales growth. Pricing-focused employees have an obligation to shine a light on the highest-impact opportunities to improve the value of the company, not just for Pricing or Finance, but for everyone who participates in determining company strategies.
- The growth mindset is what allows Pricing to uncover new possibilities and new ways to act on opportunities to grow the value of the company. Because Pricing has the ability to see beyond just the question of margins, they should lead with expansive ideas, collaborative dialogue, and illustrative communication to ensure that everyone is aligned on the best pricing strategies for achieving the company's goals.

- NEVER let another person destroy your belief in yourself or your potential. NOBODY has justifiable authority to do that. You are always right to believe in yourself. Make sure your personal role is set up for success.

In short, the growth mindset should be a prerequisite for all pricing strategy work, both as a defense against the inherent conflicts that can arise in pricing and as a powerful mental toolset for finding and implementing the best pricing strategies for any given situation.

CHAPTER 4

# The Five Sacred Metrics of Pricing Success

*What gets measured gets managed.*

—Peter Drucker (allegedly)

## Chapter Overview

In this chapter, we will discuss the **Five Sacred Metrics of Pricing Success**. Why are they sacred? Because they are UNASSAILABLE, INVIOLABLE, and highly important.

These five metrics combine to calculate the present value of all future profits of present and future customers based on sustainable rates of growth and churn—the actual **value of the company**.

1. **New Customer Revenue Acquisition Rate** (that which is repeatable)
2. **Existing Customer Revenue Expansion Rate** (that which is repeatable)
3. **Customer Revenue Churn Rate** (that which is repeatable)
4. **Annualized Profits** (that which is sustainable)
5. **Present-Value Discount Rate** (a measure of risk)

And their relationship to the value of the company is depicted in the following illustration.

## How the Five Sacred Metrics of Pricing Success Combine to Calculate Company Value

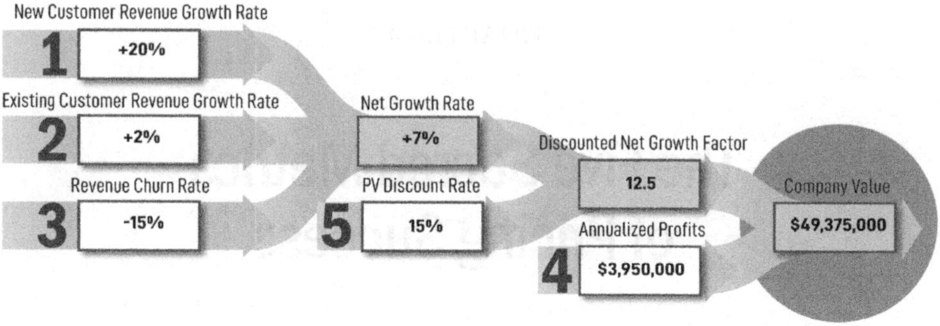


The five sacred metrics will have both forward-looking values and backward-looking values. The backward-looking values are calculated from historical transactions. They are indisputable and inarguable. Forward-looking metric values can be different than the backward-looking metrics because they must represent only what is repeatable and sustainable. They are based on what we expect. As long as we believe the backward-looking metrics are good representations of what we can expect in the future, we will use those calculated values. If not, we will need to make adjustments.

**Metric #1 - New Customer Revenue Acquisition Rate**: This is a measure of revenue from new customers, as a percentage of the previous year's total revenues. It tells you how much your new customer acquisitions are impacting your total revenues and your overall net growth rate.

**Metric #2 - Existing Customer Revenue Expansion Rate**: This is a measure of how fast you are growing revenues from your existing customers, whether from increasing customer wallet share or perhaps just from the organic growth of existing customer needs.

One caution: If your **existing customer revenue expansion rate (ECRER)** is the product of price increases, the forward-looking metric should only be representative of repeatable price increases, such as those attributable to inflation and common in the marketplace.

**Metric #3 - Customer Revenue Churn Rate:** This is the metric that helps us understand the percentage of revenues lost each year due to customers discontinuing their purchases. Again, our forward-looking metric should only include what we believe is repeatable into the future.

**Summary Metric: Net Repeatable Revenue Growth Rate:** If you add up the previous three metrics, you will have the **Net Repeatable Revenue Growth Rate**

(NRRGR). Of course, the customer revenue churn rate should be represented by a negative number.

**Metric #4 - Annualized Profits:** These are simply the profits generated by the most recent year's sales. What we care most about here is repeatability and stability. We want to make sure that there are no unexpected changes to costs or market prices as we look into the future.

WARNING: **Annualized profits** is where most companies and pricing solution providers tend to exclusively focus, mostly because it is the easiest way to show quick benefits. People have become so demanding of immediate results and payback that they are reluctant to invest in complex solutions they don't entirely understand unless they can see immediate impact on their financial statements. Generally, the easiest way to see immediate results is to raise prices because customers typically react to price increases in delayed fashion. For this reason, companies can show short-term gains in both margin percentage and overall profit dollars fairly quickly. Even though increasing prices might ultimately add unwanted risk to customer relationships, most customer defections don't occur immediately after a small price increase.

**Metric #5 – Present-Value Discount Rate:** This is the financial discount rate that is used to value future profits. It is similar to an interest rate. This rate is highly correlated with risk. In fact, this metric is ultimately a measure of both risk and the time value of money. As future profits become risk, the **present-value discount rate** (**PVDR**) will commensurately increase, and the value of future expected profits will commensurately decrease. Any pricing decision that adds risk to future profits should theoretically result in a higher **discount rate**. As you become more advanced in your strategies, you will need to reflect in your calculations how you expect pricing to affect this important metric. You can calculate an implied present-value discount rate using the other four sacred metrics and a **company value calculator**, such as

**Summary Metric: Discounted Net Growth Factor:** This key summary metric (based on the Gordon Growth Formula) combines the net repeatable growth rate with the **present-value discount rate** to produce what is essentially a profit multiple. If you multiply the **discounted net growth factor** (**DNGF**) by the annualized profits, you get the theoretical company value:

$$\text{Discounted Net Growth Factor} \times \text{Annualized Profits} = \text{Theoretical Company Value}$$

## The Sacred Pricing Metric Dashboard

The Sacred Pricing Metric Dashboard is a framework for measuring pricing results in terms of their impact on the five sacred pricing metrics. It will allow you to directly measure the impact of pricing strategies on the theoretical value of the company. I recommend creating a standard dashboard or report that includes all **five sacred metrics**, along with the **company value metric**, such as the example shown below:

**The Sacred Pricing Metric Dashboard**

| | Baseline | Year 1 | Year 2 | Year 3 | Today | Company Value Increase |
|---|---|---|---|---|---|---|
| 1 New Customer Revenue Acquisition Rate | 16.4% | 16.9% | 17.5% | 17.8% | 18.3% | +65.4% |
| 2 Existing Customer Revenue Expansion Rate | 1.1% | 1.1% | 1.3% | 1.3% | 1.5% | +13.8% |
| 3 Existing Customer Revenue Churn Rate | 8.9% | 8.9% | 8.5% | 8.4% | 8.0% | +31.0% |
| Net Repeatable Revenue Growth Rate | 8.6% | 9.1% | 10.3% | 10.7% | 11.8% | +110.2% |
| 4 Annualized Profits | $2,680,625 | $2,911,159 | $3,176,074 | $3,503,210 | $3,878,053 | +44.7% |
| 5 Present Value Discount Rate | 16% | 16% | 16% | 16% | 16% | 0% |
| Discounted Net Growth Factor | 13.5 | 14.5 | 17.5 | 18.9 | 23.8 | +110.2% |
| Company Value | $36,224,662 | $42,190,707 | $55,720,600 | $66,098,299 | $92,334,602 | +154.9% |

This particular dashboard is extremely useful because it shows the values for each of the five sacred pricing metrics, along with how each metric has contributed to the overall change in company value over time. For example, this chart shows that the improvements in new customer revenue acquisition rate roughly account for a 65.4% increase in company value.

It's important show this dashboard in meetings on pricing strategy so you can explain why it's important to "invest" in growing revenues and reducing churn.

The net growth rate is extremely important because of its compounding effect. The chart below shows the value of a company, using the Gordon growing perpetuity model, based on a discount rate (r) of 10%, a starting profit value of $100K, and various net growth rates.

**The Present Value of a $100K Growing Annuity by Growth Rate**

In $ millions

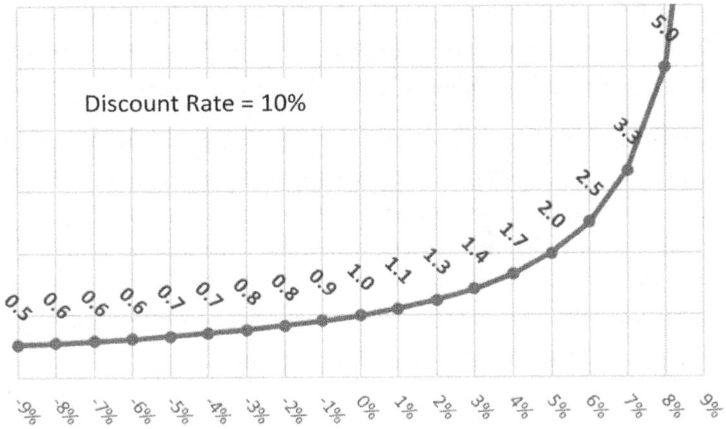


Because of the compounding effects, incrementally higher net growth rates produce exponentially higher valuations of future profits, as shown in the preceding chart.

In any case, if your overriding business objective is to maximize the value of the company, then the first point of focus should be on the metrics that have the most impact on that value.

## Chapter Summary

In this chapter, we started by defining the **five sacred metrics of pricing success** and illustrating their direct connection to the value of the company. And we pointed out some key lessons:

- In order to create pricing strategies that directly increase the value of the company, it's important to maintain visibility on all **five sacred metrics of pricing success.**
- The **pricing metric dashboard** is a critical communication tool for keeping executive attention on how pricing strategies connect to the five sacred metrics and ultimately the value of the company. It is very important to have and display that information in discussions about pricing strategy to help get people aligned with the most important opportunities.

- The most attractive opportunities to increase the value of the company can be determined by looking at the relative impact of increasing any one of the five sacred metrics, and then determining the apparent ease of accomplishing an increase to each metric. An easy way to determine this is by comparing the relative value of each metric to its respective minimum, maximum, and theoretical target value.
- The discount rate used to value future profits can be adjusted to account for different levels of uncertainty over the horizon of future profits. However, this level of sophistication is not generally required to determine good pricing strategies to maximize the value of the company.

The most important takeaway from this chapter is that company-value-maximizing pricing strategies can happen only with continuous visibility, attention, and focus on the **five sacred metrics of pricing success**. Companies that strategically prioritize their efforts, based on potential impact and opportunity, have a much better chance of making significant improvements to the overall value of their companies than those who focus randomly on one metric or attempt to improve all five metrics simultaneously.

CHAPTER 5

# The Story of Leroy Studemont

### Case Parable 2: ElastiCo and Leroy Studemont

## Chapter Overview

This chapter contains a "case parable" about Leroy Studemont, a newly hired VP of Pricing for an industrial belts company named ElastiCo. Based on his expert-level elasticity modeling and pressure from his CFO boss, he determines that raising prices by 2% (the mathematically optimized price) is the best way to maximize next year's profits, even though it means they will likely lose customers and revenues.

So they execute flawlessly a 2% price increase, and increased profits as expected. The graph below shows what happened to margins and unit sales:

**ElastiCo Unit Sales vs. Unit Margin**

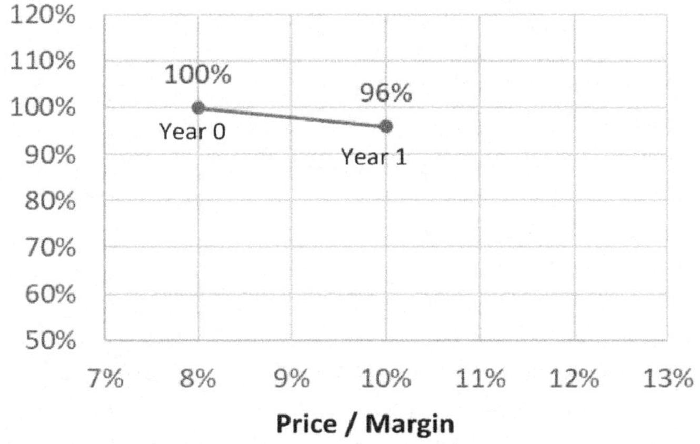

And the chart below shows what happened to revenues and profits:

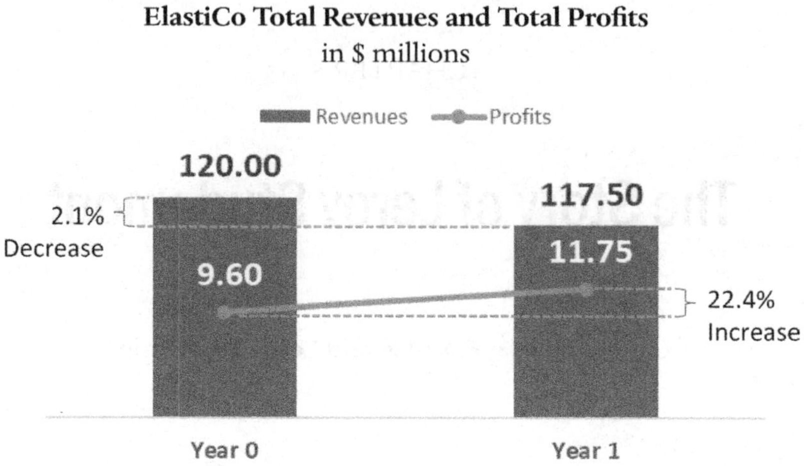


Because of the successful increase in profits based on this 2% price increase, they decided to repeat the strategy again in his second year, with similar results, as shown in the charts below:

**ElastiCo Total Revenues and Total Profits**
in $ millions

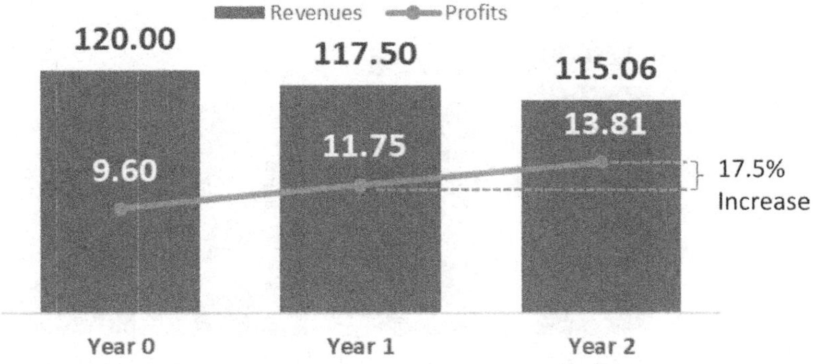


Although he was a little concerned about the continued decrease in revenues, the CFO blamed the sales shortfalls on the Sales team and said the new VP of Sales should fix it.

In the third year, Leroy repeated his analysis, but this time it showed that a 2% price increase would likely result in a 12% decrease in unit sales (due to 12% customer attrition), but it was still the "profit optimal" way to maximize profits for the next year, even though this time, profits were expected to grow by only 4.7%. The year 3 results are shown in the following charts:

**ElastiCo Unit Sales vs. Unit Margin**

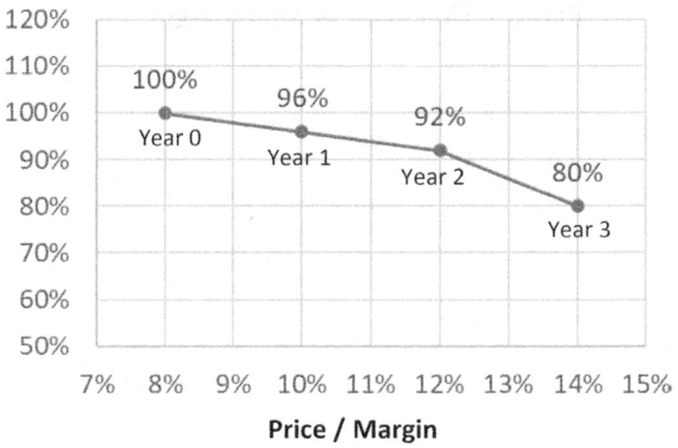

**ElastiCo Total Revenues and Total Profits**
in $ millions

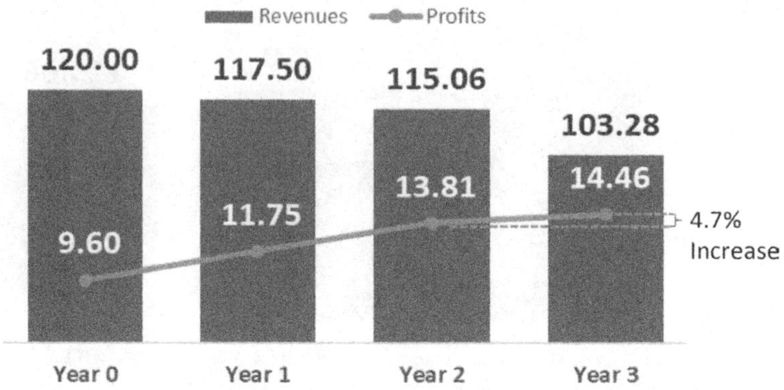


Leroy realized this strategy was not sustainable, but at this point the CFO was unwilling to lower the prices that he had just raised to increase profits, so there was pressure to continue the strategy.

Year 4's analysis showed 2% price increase would likely result in a 14% decrease in customers and unit sales, but still generate a small increase in profits. Because it was still the "profit optimal" strategy, they raised prices by 2% a fourth time. But this time the results were significantly worse than expected. Unit sales dropped by 25% (not 14% as expected), and profits fell by more than 12%. The results are shown in the charts below:

**ElastiCo Unit Sales vs. Unit Margin**

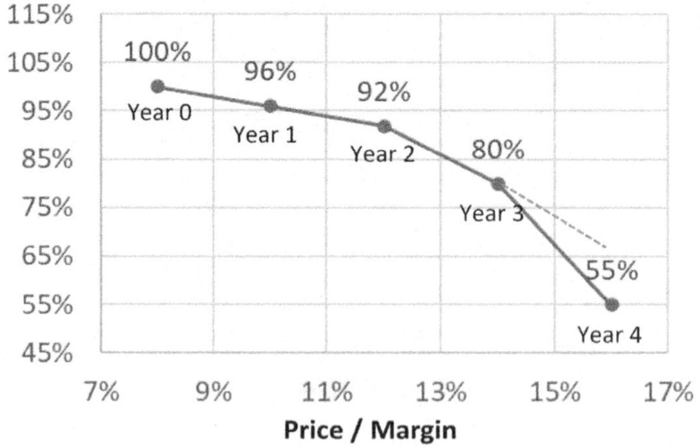

**ElastiCo Total Revenues and Total Profits**
in $ millions

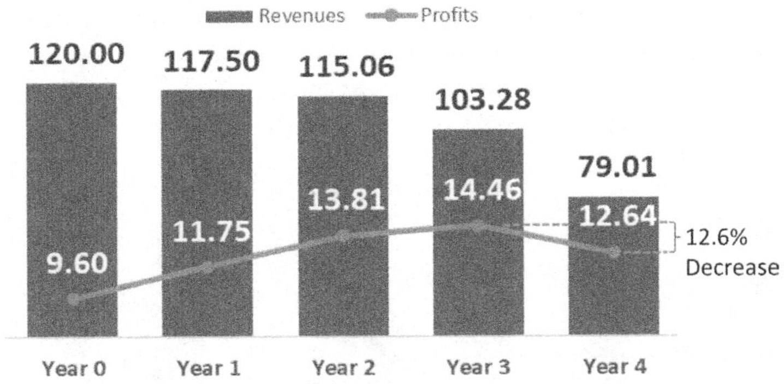


As a result of this performance, both Leroy and his CFO boss were fired. ElastiCo's stock price dropped by 33% in a single day. This resulted in a 10% layoff. Customer service quality dropped dramatically, And the remaining customers were more dissatisfied than ever.

Lucky for Leroy, all of this was just a bad dream, an omen of sorts.

So when Leroy went to his first day on the job, he was prepared to push back against his CFO boss's insistence that Leroy push prices up, explaining the long-term implications of this type of strategy. Instead, Leroy realized that they would do better to leave their prices right where they were for the next 4 years, which produced 6% growth rates that grew both revenues and profits.

This reality was much better than the alternate reality in Leroy's dream because revenues were strong, customer relationships were strong, new customer acquisitions were strong, and the company was in a much better position to succeed in the future. These actual (revised) results are shown in comparison to the (initial) results in Leroy's dream in the chart below.

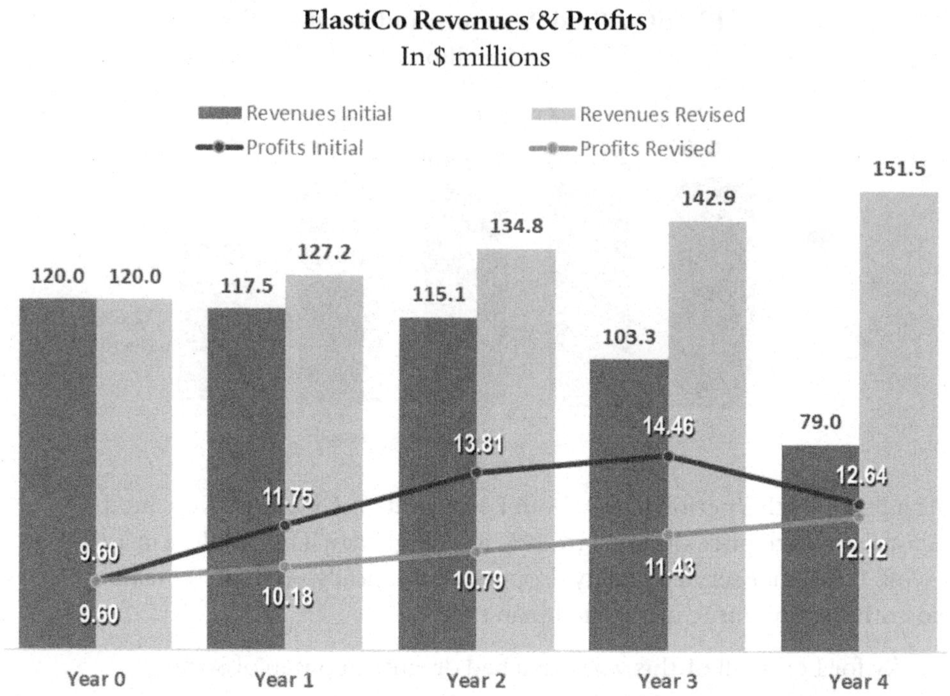


With this comparison, it's easy to see how "profit-optimal" price increase strategies can create problems for companies over the long term. Using the five sacred metrics to compare the value of the company under the two different strategies on day 1, it's easy to see that the zero-price-increase strategy led to a 3.4 times more valuable company than the 2%-price-increase strategy. Any executive could have used these metrics and tools to evaluate the value of the strategy ahead of time, using the five sacred metrics of pricing success. That's why those metrics are so important in any pricing strategy.

## Chapter Summary

This case parable illustrates some extremely important lessons about pricing strategy and customer behavior. Adhering to these lessons should help you develop the highest-value pricing strategies for your company:

- **Pay attention to all five sacred metrics.** Looking only at near-term profit results as your main metric for making pricing decisions can ultimately put your company in a dangerous position. It's imperative that you also look at how pricing decisions affect customer growth, existing-customer revenue expansion, and customer churn.

- **Annual price increases may not be sustainable sources of profit growth** (depending on what is happening to competitor or market prices). There are limits to how much you can raise prices without putting your customer relationships at risk. Raising prices puts stress on customer relationships, and if you keep applying stress to those relationships, they will eventually crumble.
- **Elasticity curves are not uniform** across the price spectrum. Customers drop off at different rates depending on the magnitude of the price increase. Make sure you are accounting for this in any elasticity model you might be tempted to use.

These lessons give us a good starting point for driving good pricing strategies. There will be other important lessons as we continue our journey through this book. But these lessons form an important foundation. If you are not currently using these concepts in developing your own pricing strategies, think of this chapter as an opportunity to make improvements that could have a big impact on the value of your company today.

PART 2

# Customer Relationships

*There is only one boss. The Customer. And he can fire everyone in the company, from the chairman on down, simply by spending his money somewhere else.*

— Sam Walton

CHAPTER 6

# Losing the Pricing Tug-O-War

*A Customer is the most important visitor on our premises.*
*He is not dependent on us. We are dependent on him.*
*He is not an interruption in our work. He is the purpose of it.*
*He is not an outsider in our business. He is a part of it.*
*We are not doing him a favor by serving him.*
*He is doing us a favor by giving us an opportunity to do so.*

—Gandhiji (Mahatma Gandhi)

## Chapter Overview

This chapter starts with the concept that long-term business success hinges on the ability to create and deliver value to the customer, something most people won't argue with. Consistent with that is the concept that adversarial customer relationships are bad for business. Yet companies often implement pricing strategies that result in adversarial relationships with their customers over price.

This situation often starts with seemingly harmless business practices that can cause a domino effect of damage to customer relationships, thereby causing damage to the company's future success. One of these business practices is the policy of discretionary discounting and negotiated prices with customers, which nearly always dominos into the **pricing tug-o-war**, where both parties focus inwardly on their own fight to get a more favorable price. This leads to a scarcity mindset and an adversarial position of win-lose propositions.

The following scenario is an example of the **pricing tug-o-war**: Imagine a company that decides to attempt a price increase. It may even do the responsible thing and notify customers. A customer then receives the notification and decides whether or not the price increase is merited. If the customer decides the price increase is not merited, they may contact the company to say they won't be buying anymore because of the price increase. Or they may say nothing, and just stop buying. When this happens, the company may agonize for a while, and then decide to offer the customer a discount or revert the price back to the previous level. Boom. A price exception is created.

But the story doesn't end there. The company now feels slighted because they had to acquiesce to the customer's will. The customer feels slighted because they had to do extra work and spend extra effort threatening to leave, just to keep the price they had before—or something close to it. Furthermore, now the customer feels less trust for the company, supposing the company will try to increase prices in the future, which means more effort they'll have to spend to fight off future price increases. The company now sees the customer as a "problem customer" because it had to spend extra effort to keep a customer who is now paying a lower ("exception") price than other customers. Now the company has to figure out a better way to raise this customer's price in the future without losing the customer, which creates more work for them, along with the possibility that this customer still might not ever accept any new, higher price.

To sum up, this activity leads to a situation where both parties feel worse off than they were before, plus now they'll have to deal with each other in the future over the issue of price. In addition, both sides feel that trust has diminished, as it becomes more clear that what the company wants and what the customer wants are not aligned. And on top of everything else, now they probably don't like each other as much as they did before. The relationship between the company and the customer has clearly worsened.

This is called the **pricing tug-o-war**. It comes in many shapes and sizes. But it always includes a company trying to increase prices and customers trying to avoid having their prices increased. It's a basic struggle over who will pocket the excess value generated in the business relationship. I call this a "win–lose game" because one side's winning is in direct proportion to the other side's losing. But in some cases, like in the example above, both sides are made worse off, and it can easily be seen as "lose–lose."

From a free-market perspective, there's nothing wrong with the pricing tug-o-war. This is exactly how mutually agreed prices get set and how trades get accomplished—buyers and sellers working in their own interests until one side concedes that the price is good enough to make the trade. In fact, many companies actively promote the pricing tug-o-war by allowing their prices to be negotiated, often based on nothing more than the random discretion of sales representatives.

The problem with the pricing tug-o-war is not that the price isn't mutually agreeable. Technically, it is mutually agreeable, or both sides wouldn't agree to make the trade. The problem is that it leads to unnecessary friction and damage to what could otherwise be a high-value business relationship between a buyer and a seller.

Contrary to what many believe, **negotiated pricing does not improve customer satisfaction**. Negotiated pricing almost always results in a situation where most customers are paying unfair prices, almost by definition, especially when the final negotiated price is based on the random discretion of an individual sales rep. In addition, "negotiated pricing" creates an unnecessary burden for the customer. The minute a customer understands that prices are negotiable, they realize they have an obligation to do more work and go through additional stress to make sure they get the best possible price. After all, the final negotiated price is a product of how much work the customer is willing to put into the negotiation. And even after all the work to negotiate, there will still be some doubt in their mind about whether or not they are overpaying.

Having to negotiate a fair price is an example of unnecessary friction in the buying process. It puts customers and sellers in adversarial positions in a zero-sum game where sellers win only when customers lose, and vice-versa.

And it only gets worse with time, as both sides try to find ways to outsmart each other, and trust continually fades away. It should be no surprise to companies who engage in negotiated pricing when their customers resort to bothersome actions designed to chip away at the company's negotiating position, such as: price complaints, shopping threats, RFPs, and constant commentary on how uncompetitive the prices are. If every aspect of the customer–vendor relationship seems like another chapter in an ongoing price negotiation, why should anyone be surprised when neither party is willing to say anything positive about the other for fear that they might somehow damage their own negotiating position?

Price negotiations lead to adversarial posturing, diminished trust, extra work, more uncertainty, skepticism regarding fair treatment, and unnecessary friction in the customer buying experience.

In a twist of irony, most companies who practice **pricing negotiation tug-o-war** with their customers usually end up with lower profit margins. Why? Because that is where they constantly draw the customer's focus and attention.

On the other hand, companies that find ways to give their customers "fair" but non-negotiable prices typically end up with higher margins. Why? Because they succeed at taking price off the table.

## The Seven Principles of Win–Win Customer Relationships

Long-term, win–win customer relationships are built on seven key principles:

1. **Trust**: Trust develops when customers believe your business strategy is aligned with their interests, and it cannot be established in any other way. Communication is the first step. The second step of building trust is never deviating from your stated strategy.
2. **Consistency**: Consistency allows customers to have faith that their expectations will be met. Consistency means minimizing surprises, either good or bad.
3. **Value Sharing**: Value sharing means consistently giving your customers more value than the money they are paying you. It means they end up *much* better off from doing business with you, not just *slightly* better off. If every transaction is priced at the very limits of their maximum willingness to pay, that means they are almost indifferent to doing the transaction.
4. **Fairness**: Fairness means you treat your customers fairly according to your own standard policies and procedures. It means you have mechanisms in place to ensure that some customers don't unfairly benefit at the expense of others.
5. **Easy and Frictionless Buying Experience**: This means you look for and remove unnecessary friction in the buying process. Since price negotiation can add friction and defeat the objective of fairness, negotiable prices should be eliminated. On the other hand, price transparency removes friction and improves the overall buying experience.
6. **Listening**: Listening is about inviting comments and questions, showing empathy, and learning about the needs of your customers. It's also about understanding your company's performance in meeting customer needs. This means having open communication channels to listen and hear what your customers have to say. It means showing respect for your customers' voices. It means following up with empathy. But most of all, it means having a process for learning from your customers.

7. **Living up to "The Promise"**: "The Promise" is what your customers expect from you based on how you communicate with them. It goes beyond that. Living up to the promise means doing what a trusting customer would expect from a responsible business owner—adhering to a standard of good business practices even if you never actually made an explicit promise to do so.

When companies adopt these principles of win–win customer relationships, it's easy to see why the pricing tug-o-war is pointless and counterproductive.

The misguided temptation to do things that remove value from customer relationships is nearsighted and generally practiced by people who don't have a long-term outlook. When you see these behaviors or attitudes occurring in your company, it should tell you something about the leaders who tolerate it. You may need to be the leader who changes it.

## Taking Price off the Table – A Necessary Foundation

There is only one way to change the mentality that allows price to be a variable of contention—take price off the table completely. Customers can never again believe that price can be negotiated with anybody—not the sales rep, not the sales VP, not the CFO, not the CEO, not the Chairman. Nobody. The number of people who have decision authority over price gets reduced to zero.

*I'm sorry, Mr. Customer, but our new lower price structure is standardized to ensure that nobody has to worry about paying a higher price than anyone else. This is good for everybody. Now all discounts are standardized based on objective criteria. Customers can get lower prices only if they meet the required volume thresholds for each discount level.*

If the customer asks who has the authority to give a lower price, the answer must be "nobody." If nobody has the authority to change the price, then it makes no sense to spend time worrying about it.

## A Benefit for All Customers vs. Any Single Customer

How do you take pricing off the table? You create a transparent and visible pricing structure, and you make it non-negotiable. You get pricing to the point that you honestly don't care if a customer leaves due to price.

This may seem counterintuitive. But it's not. The whole purpose of taking price off the table is to improve customer relationships. When you let one customer walk away because they don't get to negotiate their own exception price, you are validating and protecting your relationship with all other customers. You are refusing to let unfairness creep in and injure your relationship with those customers.

### Zero-Exception Pricing

It's called zero-exception pricing because if any one customer believes an exception is possible, and they don't receive an exception, they will be dissatisfied and believe they are not being treated fairly. This is why it's so important that nobody inside the company believes there can be any exception. If people in your company believe there might be an exception, they might inadvertently communicate this erroneous thought to the customer.

The reward? Better customer relationships, more customer trust due to pricing integrity, and increasing good will from customers based on fair and transparent pricing practices. And ultimately (and somewhat ironically) higher margins.

### Price Integrity: The Path to Transparent, Fair, and Rational Pricing

When you remove the pricing tug-o-war mentality, negotiated pricing, and exception prices, what you should be left with is **price integrity**, which will ultimately enable and ensure transparent, fair, and rational prices. It's been demonstrated across numerous studies that customers will pay more when they can trust the integrity of your prices and when they are relieved from the burden of having to negotiate.

## Chapter Summary

Let's review what we've covered in this chapter:

- Customer relationships are more valuable to companies over the long run when they are built on win–win principles, not win–lose and, for sure, not lose–lose. In order to achieve company growth goals, it's important to find ways to add value to customer relationships.
- Unfortunately, some pricing-related strategy decisions can create a domino-effect of negative experiences for the customer if you don't specifically plan to prevent them.
- Price negotiations and the tug-o-war mentality inevitably lead to adversarial positioning, unnecessary friction, negative feelings, and loss of trust in the overall customer relationship. For this reason, price negotiations should be eliminated from repeat-purchase businesses.
- Win–win customer relationships are built on the principles of trust, consistency, value sharing, fairness, easy and frictionless buying, listening, and

living up to "the promise"—**The Seven Principles of Win-Win Customer Relationships.**

- Win–win relationships require taking price off the table by making prices non-negotiable, and by using zero-exception prices that are fair, transparent, and rational.
- Discounts can be possible, but only when they are based on simple and objective criteria with a "fair" and "reasonable" rationale.

So, in one chapter, we've established some important principles of successful pricing and win–win customer relationships. We've destroyed the notion that negotiable pricing creates a positive customer buying experience. And we've established the necessity of having highly visible, transparent, and fair pricing, along with clear, simple, and reasonable discount structures, which must be based on objective and fair criteria.

CHAPTER 7

# The Importance of Trustworthy Prices

*Integrity: The choice between what's convenient and what's right.*

— Tony Dungy

## Chapter Overview

This chapter shows how and why trustworthy prices improve the value customers get from the relationship, and why customers don't mind paying higher prices when those prices exhibit **Price Integrity, Price Rationality, Price Fairness,** and **Price Transparency**. Trustworthy prices shorten the purchase decision process and improve the overall buying experience, important for maintaining the buyer inertia that keeps customers coming back over and over again.

**Price integrity** means your prices are trustworthy, incorruptible, and adherent to a stated strategy or policy determined by a repeatable process that generates consistent and defensible price outputs. It means prices are stable, justifiable, and can be trusted by customers.

Price integrity is what enables price rationality, price fairness, and ultimately price transparency. Customers value prices they can trust, and price integrity is what ensures your prices can be trusted.

**Price rationality** means prices are intentionally and logically positioned relative to each other in a way that makes sense, according to implied value or customer expectations of value:

- Products of higher perceived quality are priced higher than products of lower perceived quality.

- Products that are otherwise identical (similar quality and value), except for the color, are all given the same price.

When prices violate a customer's perceived sense of relative value, it can cause them to question the trustworthiness of your prices in general, which can then cause a devaluation of the entire customer-vendor relationship. Customers want to believe that prices make sense because, if they don't, then the customer has to do more work to ensure they are not at risk of overpaying.

**Price fairness** goes a little deeper than just a lack of "favoritism or discrimination." Most people expect a "fair" price to exhibit the following:

- It is consistent with the value being delivered.
- It is no better or worse than the price everyone else pays.
- It is based on "reasonable" profit margins.
- It is stable and doesn't change very often (in the case of market commodities the fair price is defined by a "fair margin" or a "fair premium" on top of a market cost that may fluctuate frequently.)
- It is consistent with advertised prices.
- It is not significantly out of line with other competitive market prices.

Customers value "fair" prices because it leads them to believe they are being treated fairly in other aspects of the business relationship.

**Price transparency** means your prices are visible so all customers can see them. When companies make prices visible and transparent, they are conveying to the world that there are no secrets, and that they plan to honor the same prices for all customers. The easiest way to make prices transparent is to display prices on your website.

Price transparency is a public confession of price integrity, price rationality, and price fairness. It gives customers reassurance that they don't have to worry about price.

## Markdowns

Many companies have a practice of marking down the prices of products, temporarily, for the purpose of moving excess inventory or trying to stimulate demand for slow-moving products. It is possible to offer markdowns to customers in a way that improves customer trust and good will and also preserves price integrity as long as:

- Customers understand and expect markdowns in a particular industry as a way of moving excess inventory and stimulating demand.

- Customers receive advance notice that markdowns are coming on a certain date in order to prevent a situation where a customer pays full price for a product, and then finds out two days later that they could have saved a lot of money if they had waited.
- Customers are offered a time-based price guarantee to give the assurance that they won't miss an opportunity to save money.
- Markdown discounts are made available to all customers who objectively qualify.

### Standardized Discounts Based on Objective Criteria

Sometimes you have to have the ability to charge different prices for different customers, perhaps based on the volume or type of business they do with your company. By structuring discounts as **standardized programs** with **objective criteria** for eligibility, you will be able to still engender trust and good will with your customers.

It is perfectly okay to create standardized discount structures as long as you keep to the following guidelines:

1. Discounts must be simple and understandable.
2. Discounts must be based on objective criteria.
3. Discounts must be based on a "fair" and "reasonable" rationale, meaning the reason for the discount makes sense and seems fair and not discriminatory.

Discount structures can be in the form of on-invoice discounts or post-purchase rebates. Sometimes the post-purchase rebates have more advantages than on-invoice discounts because they allow the discounts to be somewhat distanced from the customer's perception of price.

It's also important to ensure that discount structures don't incentivize customers to behave irrationally. For example, a discount for new customers should not make existing customers upset or regret being loyal customers.

## Chapter Summary

In this chapter, we've covered the importance of price integrity, price rationality, price fairness, and price transparency in order to create good will with your customers and improve their buying experience. We also talked about temporary markdowns to move excess or slow-moving inventory and what guidelines should be followed to avoid the destruction of good will we built through fair and transparent pricing. And finally, we talked about standardized discount structures that allow for designed price differentiation based on objective eligibility criteria, along with the key guidelines for making them effective.

Key takeaways from this chapter include the following:

- **Customers value price integrity and transparency** because it removes a burden and makes their buying experience more pleasant and efficient, and as a result they are willing to pay more for the same products—on average, as much as 5% more. This alone can be a differentiator that makes customers want to buy from you vs. a competitor.
- **Price integrity** means there is a rationale or reason behind your prices, and you have a repeatable process for determining prices and achieving consistent outputs. Price integrity means your prices are incorruptible, and they can be trusted.
- **Price rationality** means your prices make sense in terms of their relative position to the prices of other related products and services.
- **Price fairness** means the price is generally in line with the value delivered to the customer, is no more or less than what other customers pay, is generally in line with competitive market prices, does not result in unreasonably high profit margins, and is consistent with what the company has previously advertised.
- **Price transparency** means prices are freely visible for all to see, as a demonstration that there are no hidden or secret prices, as everything is out in the open.
- **Markdowns** can be possible without undermining consistent, rational, fair, and transparent prices if they are communicated ahead of time to give customers the chance to alter their purchases to take advantage. But the best way to keep customers from having to worry about price is through a generous time-based price guarantee policy.
- **Standardized discount programs** can coexist without undermining transparent price integrity as long as they are: based on objective eligibility criteria, simple to understand, and based on fair and reasonable rationales that don't incentivize irrational customer behavior that can degrade the customer relationship.

The last two chapters have shown problems that can be created in customer relationships when companies allow the pricing tug-o-war mentality, the practice of price negotiations, and the lack of fair and trustworthy pricing to create unnecessary burdens for customers.

The solution to these problems is to move to standardized, zero-exception pricing that is rational, fair, and transparent along with standardized discount programs based on objective eligibility criteria. Doing this will allow companies to "take price off the table," resulting in better customer buying experiences, improved customer relationships, and higher overall margins. This will translate to lower churn and greater predictability of growth and retention rates, some of the most important and sacred pricing metrics leading to increased company value.

CHAPTER 8

# The Chronicles of Sara's Pricing Overhaul

**Case Parable 3: FriendlyCo and New CEO, Sara Thompson**

## Chapter Overview

This chapter is a case parable of FriendlyCo, a $500 million provider of chemicals and plastics for injection-mold manufacturing. After four years of below-average margins and struggling profitability, the board of directors fired the old CEO and brought in an up-and-coming industry leader, Sara Thompson, from one of the company's stronger competitors. Her primary mission as the new CEO was to increase profitability and help the company get back on a growth trajectory.

What she found in her first days as CEO included the following:

- The company had 150 salespeople who all had pricing authority, and whose commissions were calculated based on gross sales revenue.
- Wide price variations—up to 50% or more on most products. This meant that one customer might be paying $600 per unit, while another customer might be paying over $900 for exactly the same product.
- Low margins: 20% of the Sales-negotiated transactions were below costs, and 70% of prices were below the standard industry average margin of 15%.
- No standardized criteria for discounts. It seemed like the only determinant of pricing was the customer's willingness or unwillingness to pay higher prices, or worse, the sales rep's willingness to give discounts.

Pricing and Sales leaders described their pricing strategy as follows: They wanted to capture as high a price as the customer was willing to pay, and so they asked their sales reps to start out quoting the unrealistically high "list prices," typically based on a 50% gross margin, and then negotiate down as necessary to win the business. Sales reps were told not to go below break-even, unless they felt they were at risk of losing the customer, in which case they would consult a manager for special approval.

When Sara asked how their customers felt about their final negotiated prices, her leaders admitted that their customers never really seemed happy with the prices they had negotiated. "They usually act like they are somehow doing us a favor to agree to prices above what they thought was fair," said one of the sales managers. Somehow the customers seemed to feel adversarial about the whole process.

When Sara asked how the customers felt about the quality of the products and services, she learned that the customers were reluctant to say anything positive about them, almost like they wanted the right to complain in future price negotiations to get a better price.

Sara then asked how the salespeople felt about the customers. Her leaders confessed that the salespeople generally had a bad attitude about the customers, because the ones that weren't dumb enough to pay list prices cut into their commissions by negotiating lower prices. They believed that if the list-price customers ever found out how much they were paying over regular market prices, they would get angry and leave.

After these discussions, Sara realized FriendlyCo had a massive pricing problem which was causing adversarial and risky relationships with their customers which were spiraling downward much too fast. So, Sara took a page from her previous company's book, and determined she had to change the pricing strategy.

## The New Pricing Strategy

Sara realized that even though the existing pricing practices were not good for either customers or employees, she would likely receive lots of pushback. But she knew that if she could get the company to use a new and better pricing strategy, both the company and its customers would be better off in the long run, and they would be able to replace any customers they lost in the process.

The new pricing strategy would have the following pillars:

- **No More Negotiated Prices**: All prices would be determined by the Pricing team and be take-it-or-leave-it.
- **Price Transparency**: All prices would be posted on the company's website, along with a notice that the company was moving to an everyday-low-price strategy.
- **"Fair Pricing" Commitment**: On the website, and on all quotes, the company would publish their commitment to "fair pricing," which included the following bullet points:
    1. Every customer would pay a fair price, no better or worse than what all other customers were paying.
    2. All prices would be posted on the website, so all customers would have full knowledge of all prices for all products.
    3. Any discount incentives would be based on objective criteria and open to all customers who qualified.
    4. Price changes would happen no more frequently than once every 90 days.
    5. The company would seek to keep prices competitive with similar quality products and services in the market.
- **Zero Exceptions**: Other than the pricing committee, nobody in the company would have authority to change prices, not even Sara.
- **Market-Relevant Prices**: List prices would be set 5% above market, so with standardized discounts, they would be selling near regular market rates.

In order to prepare for the massive transformation, the company would undertake the following:

1. **Focus on customer experience/no service failures**: The intent would be to minimize service failures to aggravate customer attitudes even more during this period of changing pricing policies.
2. **A highly visible and publicized change in pricing strategy**: The company would highlight major benefits to the customers of the new pricing strategy, including fairness, transparency, stability, etc. It was important for the company to control the message.
3. **Customers would not be made worse off in the short term**: Customers would receive temporary discounts to make sure that the new pricing strategy would not result in significantly higher prices for at least the next 90 days.

4. **New prices highly visible**: New pricing would be highly visible to customers on all sales quotes and invoices for the next 180 days, and all major communications would include a link to the public price lists on the website.
5. **No negotiations, no exceptions**: It was critical that people both inside and outside the company believed that pricing was not up for discussion.

With these five principles, Sara believed the needed transition had a good chance to be successful.

## Preparing for the Transition

To prepare for the transition, the Pricing team created a simple volume-based discount model which offered three tiers of discount, as follows:

| Annualized Spend (based on last three months of purchases) | Discount off List Price |
|---|---|
| \$20,000–\$50,000/year | 5% off |
| \$50,000–\$150,000/year | 7.5% off |
| Greater than \$150,000/year | 10% off |

These discount tiers were chosen because they overlapped nicely with existing customer prices, leaving very few exceptions. By comparing the new pricing with existing customer pricing, they found customers generally fell into one of three groups:

**Group 1 (Benefiters):** New prices generally better than previous prices. No problems foreseen.

**Group 2 (Same Ballpark):** New prices were roughly the same as the old prices with some higher and some lower, but generally all within 5% difference between new and old prices.

**Group 3 (Negative Impact):** New prices were generally worse than the existing negotiated prices, but the magnitude was generally 10% or lower, meaning a 10% additional discount would make them better off.

Sara was most concerned about Group 3 because they stood to lose the most, and she considered making the "transitional loyalty discount" available only to those select customers. But after further consideration, she realized that offering it to everyone would help reinforce the idea that nobody would receive preferential treatment, so that's what she decided to do.

## Additional Transitional Loyalty Discount

Sara and her Pricing team decided to offer a **Transitional Loyalty Rebate Credit** for five quarters, for customers that continued purchasing at roughly the same rate (at least 90% of their average quarterly volume), starting with 10% the first quarter, and decreasing the rebate by 2% each quarter. Because the rebate credit was a single lump sum at the end of the quarter, it was sufficiently disconnected from the actual product prices that it would allow the customers to get accustomed to the new pricing structure. It was big enough that customers would take it seriously. It was structured so that it would die down over time, as customers became more entrenched in their purchase habits under the new pricing schema.

## The Rollout

It took Sara and her team 90 days to complete the preparations to make the pricing change, including the posting of all the new information on the website. During these 90 days, each sales rep met with their customers to explain the change that was coming. As expected, even though most customers stood to benefit, at least in the short term, there was a lot of complaining, and several customers threatened to leave if they experienced a material price increase.

Finally, the day came, and the new prices and policies went into effect. To everyone's surprise, orders continued to flow in at about the same rate as before. And this repeated throughout the rest of the quarter.

At the end of the first quarter, sales were up 12% after near zero growth for the previous 16 quarters. The growth was due to new online customers who were not buying before because the list prices were too high.

Even more surprising, pre-rebate profit margins were up 8%. Of course, there was a new rebate liability that needed to be factored in. But even that wasn't enough to offset the margin increases. In the first quarter after the transition, 72% of the customers were eligible for the rebate because they had purchased a greater dollar volume than the previous quarter. That meant roughly a 7.2% hit to margins after the fact. They still ended up with a 0.8% profit margin increase over prior quarters, and they accomplished this with 12% quarter-over-quarter sales growth.

The next four quarters were equally impressive in both sales growth and profit margins, as shown in the table below:

| Quarter | Sales Growth QoQ | Incremental GM% Growth | Cumulative GM% Growth | Rebate Credit Offset | Net Profit % Growth |
|---|---|---|---|---|---|
| Qtr #1 | +12.0% | +8.0% | +8.0% | -7.2% | +0.8% |
| Qtr #2 | +2.0% | +1.6% | +9.6% | -5.1% | +4.5% |
| Qtr #3 | +3.5% | +1.3% | +10.9% | -3.7% | +7.2% |
| Qtr #4 | +2.3% | +1.2% | +12.1% | -2.2% | +9.9% |
| Qtr #5 | +3.4% | +0.9% | +13.0% | -1.1% | +11.9% |
| Total | +23.2% | +13.0% | +13.0% | - | +13.0% |

Over the entire five-month transition, FriendlyCo grew sales by 23.2% (18.5% annualized growth rate) and grew margins by 13 percentage points, which was a 191% increase over the 6.8% margins the company had been getting when Sara first arrived.

## The Long-Term Results

Over the next couple of years, FriendlyCo maintained 18% annual sales growth rates and held margin percentage steady at approximately 19%. The valuation of the company went through the roof. The stock price increased by 450%. The **five sacred metrics of pricing success** show how much the theoretical valuation of the company improved from the day Sara arrived (T0) to the completion of the pricing transition, which lasted five quarters (T+5 qtrs), as shown in the table below:

**FriendlyCo Pricing Metric Performance Before and After**

| Metric Comparison | Before ($T_0$) | After (T+5 qtrs) |
|---|---|---|
| Annualized Revenue | $500 million | $616 million |
| New Customer Revenue Acquisition Rate | +6% | +21% |
| Existing Customer Revenue Expansion Rate | 0% | 2% |
| Customer Revenue Churn Rate | -6% | -5% |
| Net Revenue Growth Rate | 0% | 18% |
| Annualized Profits | $34 million | $117 million |
| Present-Value Discount Rate | 20% | 20% |
| Discounted Net Growth Factor | 5X | 50X |
| Company Value | $170 million | $5.8 billion |

The theoretical value of the company increased by 3400%, much more than the 450% increase in the actual stock price. But Sara was confident that if they could continue this performance for another couple of years, the market would continue to reward the company with a much higher stock price.

In addition to the financial metrics, life was significantly better for FriendlyCo's customers and sales reps. More customers were happy with the service they received, and they actually left glowing reviews on social media. The adversarial customer–sales rep relationships of the past completely vanished. Customers had more honest and productive interactions with the company, which helped FriendlyCo make changes to their service offerings and customer experiences, resulting in increased customer loyalty.

## Chapter Summary

The FriendlyCo parable illustrates some important points that are applicable to many different businesses:

- Negotiated pricing, based on unrealistic list prices and lack of price transparency, can create adversarial and high-risk customer relationships and lead to low levels of customer satisfaction.
- Sometimes drastic changes need to be made to pricing structures and strategies in order to overcome stalled growth and unhappy customers.
- Seemingly impossible changes to pricing and customer policies CAN be accomplished. And when teams are well prepared, it can be done with minimal negative effect.
- The five sacred metrics of pricing success should be the gauge to measure the benefits of new pricing strategies and how they will ultimately affect the value of the company.
- Major changes to pricing strategies and structures MUST include mitigations for inevitable disruptions to customer buying inertia. Often, customers must receive something of extra value to offset the unavoidable negative effects of the change. However, these extra benefits can be short-term benefits that only last until the customers' new habits are formed, and then they can be slowly tapered off.
- Discounts or rewards intended to compensate customers during the period of pricing changes should be sufficiently disconnected, so customers get the experience and feel of the new, permanent pricing and discount policies.

- Removing destructive pricing policies and practices will often unlock potential sources of growth and profitability. This can help offset any negative effects from the change.

Like many companies, FriendlyCo had many dysfunctional customer relationships based on a lack of price integrity and the adversarial nature of the pricing tug-o-war along with the burden of negotiated prices. Although the business had been stagnant for a few years, it was full of customer relationship risk, which ultimately could have caused even bigger problems for the company. The only way to fix the mess was to massively overhaul their pricing strategies and practices.

But most companies in this situation are too reluctant to make the necessary changes because they are worried about the one-time transformation risk. The problem with this thinking is that the one-time transformation risk can be mitigated and managed, whereas the long-term risk to the business of not making the change is potentially fatal. The mitigation to that risk is to make the change to healthier pricing practices.

CHAPTER 9

# The Age of Millennials

*Millennials are more aware of society's many challenges than previous generations and less willing to accept maximizing shareholder value as a sufficient goal for their work.*

—Michael Porter

## Chapter Overview

This chapter is about the current digital revolution and the two major forces driving it—the momentum of new technological capabilities and the coming-of-age of a new generation of Millennial buyers. As of 2020, Millennials make up 50% of the global workforce. Experts say that by 2025, Millennials will make up 75% of the global workforce. That means, for the next two decades, most B2B purchases will be decided by Millennials. Compared to previous generations, Millennials seem to have different personal values, leading to different considerations in the way they make decisions, as summarized below:

1. **Trust, Transparency, and Authenticity**: More than other generations, Millennials value trust and authenticity and expect transparency in their relationships. Skeptical of hype and buzzwords, they more often defer to personal experiences or reviews based on the experiences of others.
2. **Social Connectedness and Collaboration**: Millennials are highly connected on social networks, and they value collaboration with others in their networks. They share their experiences with others. They socialize their buying decisions as well as their consumption.

3. **Ethical Values and Social Responsibility**: Millennials are generally more socially progressive, with concern about the environment, social equality, diversity, and corporate social responsibility, preferring to support businesses that care about the same causes they care about.
4. **Curiosity and Self-Education**: They are curious, industrious, and capable of processing decisions based on their own research. They are digitally connected and tech savvy. They embrace innovations and new ideas, and they don't feel anchored to previous generations' beliefs.
5. **Experientiality and Skepticism**: In contrast to their predecessors in Generation X, Millennials value experiences more than "things." And they value the experiences of others as well. In this vein, they leverage reviews from others to make purchasing decisions.
6. **Impatient and Expectant of Instant Response**: As a result of the instant gratification they've had in many areas of their lives, they generally expect instantaneous responses to online queries and product questions. They expect products and technology to work without problems, and they have very little tolerance for products or technologies that don't.
7. **Creative, Entrepreneurial, and Independent**: Millennials don't like being under the control and influence of corporate structures and hierarchies. They have very little loyalty to companies, and they value the freedom to move from opportunity to opportunity. Although they are achievement oriented, they care more about doing meaningful work than they care about maximizing shareholder value.
8. **Frugal, Practical, and Efficient**: Millennials are generally more frugal than the prior generation. They are more attracted to practical and simplified lifestyles than flamboyant overconsumption. They prefer fast and efficient communication in short bursts, like text messages, tweets, and social media posts, rather than longer emails, phone calls, or meetings. Millennials are multitaskers. Because of this, they can sometimes be easily distracted. But they are also typically open and adaptive to change.

It is clear that we are seeing a generational shift in B2B buying behaviors based on both the unique characteristics of Millennials and the broader availability of e-commerce. Companies should consider the following modifications to their pricing strategies, based on the growing influence of Millennials:

1. **Keep Pricing Ethical:** Or Millennials won't want to have anything to do with your company, just on the principle of it.
2. **Move to Transparent Pricing:** Millennials will be skeptical of companies who don't post pricing.

3. **Keep Pricing Structures Simple:** Millennials don't have time for unnecessary complexity.
4. **Ensure Consistent and Fair Pricing across Customers**: Remember, millennials are connected, and they talk.
5. **Avoid Bait and Switch Pricing Practices**: This is a breach of trust, and Millennials will talk.
6. **Eliminate High-Pressure Sales Tactics**: Millennials are capable of making their own decisions based on their own research, and they know more than you might suspect.
7. **Get Rid of Negotiated Prices**. Millennials don't need another way to waste time in the buying process, and negotiations imply lack of fairness.
8. **Keep Customer Communication Channels Open**: They're already talking. Make it easy for them to talk with you.

The wave of millennial buyers is changing the way companies must compete for business. By getting ahead of this trend and incorporating this knowledge into your pricing strategies, you will position yourself to win against your competitors who react more slowly.

## Chapter Summary

The rise of Millennials, in combination with the ongoing transition to digital commerce, means that your customers are changing. The new generation of millennial customers have different behaviors, expectations, and values than prior customers, and it's advantageous to understand these differences while constructing pricing strategies and go-to-market plans.

The new millennial characteristics include:

1. Trust, transparency, and authenticity
2. Social connectedness and collaboration
3. Ethical values and social responsibility
4. Curiosity and self-education
5. Experientiality and skepticism
6. Impatient and expectant of instant response
7. Creative, entrepreneurial, and independent
8. Frugal, practical, and efficient

These characteristics suggest that pricing strategies should be modified to accommodate these general characteristics of the millennial generation with eight specific considerations:

1. Keep pricing ethical.
2. Move to transparent pricing.
3. Keep pricing structures simple.
4. Ensure consistent and fair pricing across customers.
5. Avoid bait-and-switch pricing practices.
6. Eliminate high-pressure sales techniques.
7. Get rid of negotiated prices.
8. Keep customer communication channels open.

These suggestions should help you be more successful as the millennial generation takes over most B2B purchasing (and B2C purchasing as well) in the next few years, especially if you make adaptive changes more quickly than your competitors.

And even if you haven't seen signs of the described millennial characteristics in your business in recent years, it is likely things will change. What created success in the past and what will create success in the future are not always the same. More commonly, success comes to those who can effectively adapt to change.

CHAPTER 10

# Your Key Customer Categories

*Understanding human needs is half the job of meeting them.*

—Adlai Ewing Stevenson II

## Chapter Overview

In order to understand the most lucrative opportunities for growing the value of your company, it's important to first understand your customers—who they are, how they shop, how frequently they buy from you, and how fast they move through the **natural customer lifecycle**. With this knowledge, you can better understand how you are doing at attracting, retaining, and growing your customer relationships.

It's important to understand customer loyalty and why it exists. In most cases, "loyalty" is a misnomer. Loyalty implies that a customer has some sort of underlying commitment to a company, but this is not typically what happens in business relationships. Customers almost always behave in their own self-interest. What may appear to be loyalty is usually nothing more than cost avoidance.

**Customer loyalty** is greater when a greater amount of costs can be avoided by consolidating purchases with a single vendor. When a customer has multiple repeat purchases to make, purchasing from a single or small number of vendors can reduce overall **evaluation costs, transaction costs, fulfillment costs,** or **switching costs**. Understanding customer loyalty means understanding the customer attributes that drive customer loyalty, which are:

- **Repeat-Purchase Needs:** When customers need to make lots of repeat purchases, there is a greater opportunity to find cost savings by purchasing from a single vendor.
- **Evaluation Costs**: Customers will be more loyal when there are significant costs to evaluating other vendors and/or solutions. Customers who don't care about the differences in products or services tend to have lower evaluation costs because there is less to evaluate, and customers who find it easy to evaluate other solutions tend to be less loyal.
- **Transaction Costs**: Customers tend to be more loyal when transactions costs are high because they will seek to consolidate these costs with a single vendor. Transaction costs include any cost or effort required by customers to get through the purchase process once a decision has been made, including anything from the initial costs of setting up an account to the process of ordering, purchasing, billing, credit processing, setting up payment terms, tracking orders, etc.
- **Fulfillment Costs**: When fulfillment costs are high (with other vendors), customers tend to be more loyal to a single vendor where they can consolidate or avoid those costs to deliver, install, and implement purchases. Customers who are geographically isolated tend to have higher shipping or fulfillment costs.
- **Switching Cost**: Customers tend to be more loyal when switching costs are high. This can include any costs customers experience when switching between one vendor and another, including learning about new products, new shopping and ordering procedures, or new support structures. It can include the cost of retooling systems, entering and managing new sets of data, changing product specs, or informing customers of new products and features.

The more these attributes are prevalent in your industry and with your customers, the more customer loyalty you should expect under regular circumstances.

In addition, there could be other potential characteristics or attributes, such as **size, geography, industry,** or **amount of annual purchases,** which can be used to identify customer loyalty or price sensitivity. What's important is to understand how and why those attributes affect the customer's ability to minimize costs.

## Relationship Buyers (and Other Buyer Types)

Most repeat customers are **relationship buyers** (vs. **product-level buyers** or **cart-level buyers**). This is important to understand because, for **relationship buyers**, the price of an individual product or service almost doesn't matter, as long as it's not flagrantly out of line. **Relationship buyers** expect that overall pricing will generally be in the ballpark of what is "fair," and they will focus on other aspects of the overall relationship, especially those things that help reduce evaluation costs, transaction costs, and fulfillment costs.

There are three different buyer profile types:

**Product-level buyers** make a separate buying decision for each product they buy. If they have three products to buy, they will make three different vendor decisions. What makes them product-level buyers is typically the ease with which they can shop and compare prices at the individual product level and the potential savings they can achieve from buying from several different vendors.

**Cart-level buyers** may shop with a few different vendors to see who generally has the most attractive prices, but after they've shopped, they buy most or all of their desired products from the same vendor. For them, shopping is relatively easy, but they don't like the hassle of dealing with many different vendors for similar types of orders (usually due to high transaction and fulfillment costs), so they generally choose one vendor for the whole cart (of related purchases).

**Relationship buyers** make up the majority of repeat-purchase customers. They typically don't like to shop for price because it's relatively costly in terms of time and effort, and price is only one aspect of the vendor relationship. Instead, they prefer to find fewer vendors that can serve a high volume of their needs at a "fair" price. They typically build vendor-specific habits for ordering and searching for products they need. This is how they keep transaction costs low—by forming efficient processes around purchasing from a few key vendors. Relationship buyers value the elements of the relationship that contribute to the ease of doing business, including knowledge of what to expect in terms of timing, delays, support, etc.

Anytime you have entrenched buyer inertia and significant switching costs, you have a relationship buyer. That means **repeat purchasers** and **relationship buyers** are generally one and the same. Therefore, the easiest way to determine if you have relationship buyers is to look in your transactions to see if you have **regular repeat buyers**—customers who purchase frequently and regularly. From their purchase behavior, you can infer the many other attributes that are often associated with relationship buyers.

**Relationships buyers** get many tangible and intangible benefits from their repeat-purchase relationships. **Relationship buyers** usually develop very entrenched buyer inertia to the extent that they would bear significant switching costs if they were to move to another vendor. Once customers have established entrenched buying habits, for better or for worse, price doesn't seem to have as much impact on purchasing decisions as other factors.

## The Natural Velocity of Your Business

**Business velocity** refers to the frequency with which typical repeat customers make purchases, ranging from daily to once per year. Understanding the typical frequency of customer purchases is critical for interpreting customer behavior signals. For example, if you have a customer who hasn't purchased in three weeks, how do you know if you should you be concerned? If your business velocity is monthly, you probably have nothing to worry about. However, if your business velocity is daily, then three weeks without a purchase probably means something is wrong. A simple way to estimate your business velocity is to count all purchases by repeat customers and then divide 365 days by that number to get your average purchase interval (in days).

Doing this for all your customers will give you great insight into your customers, using a frequency chart like the one below:

**Number of Customers by Average Interval Between Purchases**

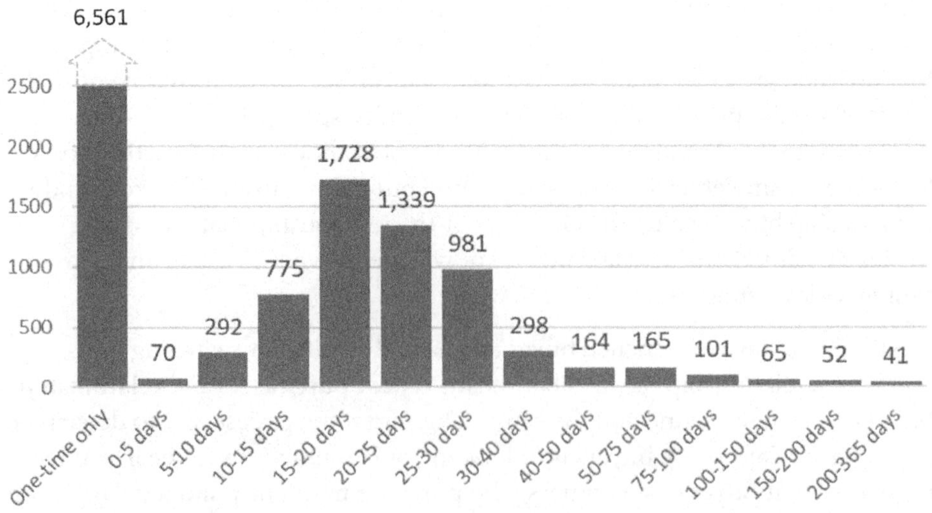

In this chart, the largest single bucket of customers has a purchase interval between 15 and 20 days. But it's easy to see, also, that there are significant volumes of repeat-purchase customers in the range of 10–15 days, 20–25 days, and 25–30 days. The vast majority of repeat-purchase customers would be covered by describing the typical repeat customer purchase interval as ranging between 10 and 30 days. The velocity of this example business seems to be closest to monthly—meaning customers typically make a purchase at least once per month.

After determining your natural business velocity, you can use this information to define the stages in your customer lifecycle model. Below is a generic customer lifecycle model that can be used for most businesses:

**Universal Customer Lifecycle Model for Repeat-Purchase Businesses**

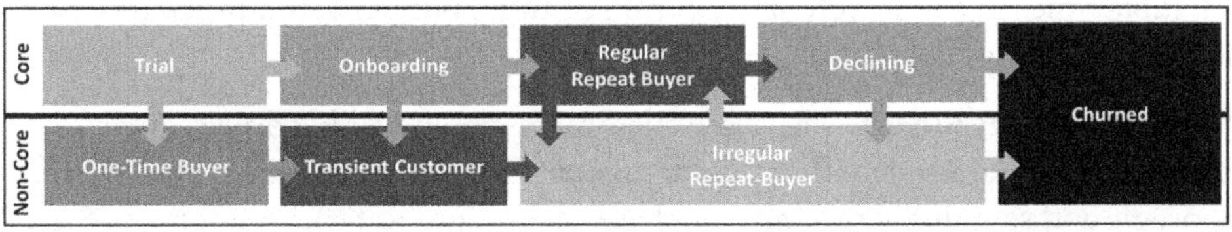


The arrows show the typical flow of how customers can move through the lifecycle model depending on their purchase behavior. The first five stages are called **core stages** because they include the expected path of "**core**" customers. **Core customers** are customers who are an ideal fit for your business—the ones that you hope will eventually become **regular repeat buyers**. **Non-core customers** include one-time buyers or irregular repeat buyers who are not on a path to likely become **regular repeat buyers**. Below are the major stages in the universal customer lifecycle model.

## Core Stages

**Trial** (**New**): These are customers who have made a single purchase commitment. They don't yet have any behavioral inertia compelling them to buy more. They are forming impressions about your company.

**Onboarding** (**New**): These are customers who have passed the trial period and are starting to make recurring purchases with your company. Because they have begun making repeat purchases, it can be presumed that they have at least a mild intention of continuing to do business with you, as long as everything goes well.

**Regular** (**Onboarded**) **Repeat Buyers**: These are customers who have established sufficiently entrenched buying habits that they naturally continue to buy from you on a regular basis. This is the customer lifecycle stage in which most companies want their customers to stay.

**Declining**: These are customers who were at one time **regular repeat buyers** but who have recently slowed down or stopped purchasing for a period of time called the **buffer period**.

**Churned**: These are customers who were once repeat buyers, but who stopped purchasing altogether for the duration of the buffer period and have crossed the **churn threshold** (typically 4–12 months of no purchases).

## Non-Core Stages

**One-Time**: These are customers who purchase only once.

**Transient Repeat Buyers**: These are **repeat customers** who may purchase multiple times in a relatively short period of time, but then stop purchases for a long period of time.

**Irregular Repeat Buyers**: These are customers who never become regular customers with entrenched repeat buying patterns. Instead, they make sporadic and seemingly random purchases from time to time. Sometimes these customers are loyal customers of the competition.

It's important to understand the make up of your regular revenues, so you can set improvement goals and estimate the impact of new pricing strategies. The chart below shows a company where regular repeat customers make up the bulk of the revenues and profits.

**Total Current Year Revenue by Customer Lifecycle Stage**

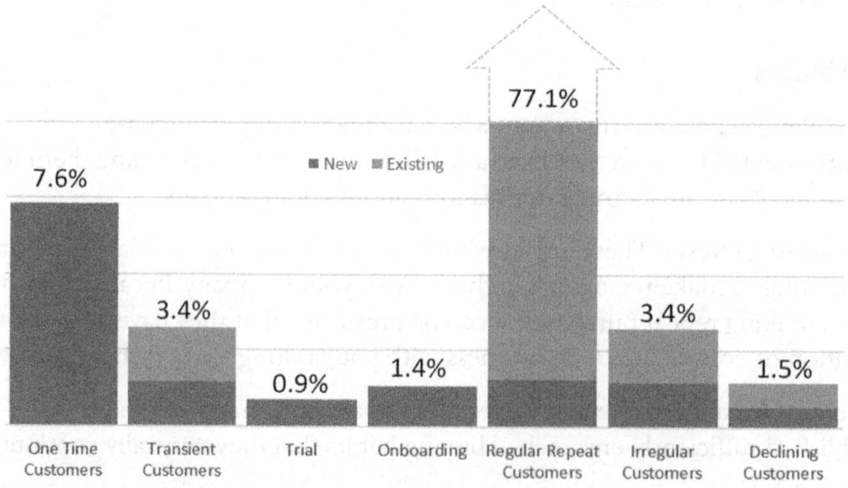

Dividing customers into segments based on their current customer lifecycle stage is a good way to see opportunities for growth.

## The Five Basic Customer-Loyalty Profiles of Repeat Buyers

Almost all repeat-purchase businesses have a mix of loyalty among their repeat customers. The **five basic customer-loyalty profiles** introduced here are helpful for recognizing different types of repeat customers, so you can effectively create strategies for acquiring, retaining, and growing high-value customer relationships.:

**Unprofitable Bottom Feeders (irregular repeat customers)**: These are the customers you generally don't want. They only buy at prices below your profitability threshold. Chasing after these customers doesn't make any sense.

**Opportunistic Customers (irregular repeat customers)**: These customers have no significant buyer inertia, loyalty, or switching costs. They buy from you when your price is relatively attractive, but they recognize value.

**Light Inertia Customers (regular repeat buyers)**: These customers have a habit and pattern of behavior which includes buying from you. And while they are not likely to leave due to mild changes in price or mild service disruptions, any significant disruption or price increase (e.g., 5% or greater) would likely result in significant attrition risk.

**Heavy Inertia Customers (regular repeat buyers)**: These customers have entrenched buyer inertia and significant switching costs, and they are not likely to leave unless there is a major service disruption or a significant price increase. Often, these customers have built businesses around their chosen vendors, so they are not even looking at other vendors seriously.

**Captive or Die-Hard Customers**: These customers will not leave until your price or service hits some extreme level of unreasonableness because their reasons for buying from you go far beyond price. They are willing to pay high—even "unfair"—prices because they value your products and services and/or the business relationship much more highly than the price of the transactions.

It's important to understand the composition of your repeat-purchase customer base. If your customer base is mostly made up of high-inertia and die-hard customers, then you probably have extremely low risk of churn. Your best opportunities might be found in attracting and onboarding new customers. On the other hand, if most of your customers are in the opportunistic or low-inertia profiles, you may want to focus on opportunities to prevent churn and to increase customer buying inertia and switching costs by solidifying the long-term value proposition of doing business with you.

When you overlay the customer loyalty profiles, you get a multi-dimensional view of your customers, which can help you visually understand how customers move through the customer lifecycle:

**Customer Lifecycle Map (with Basic Loyalty Profiles)**

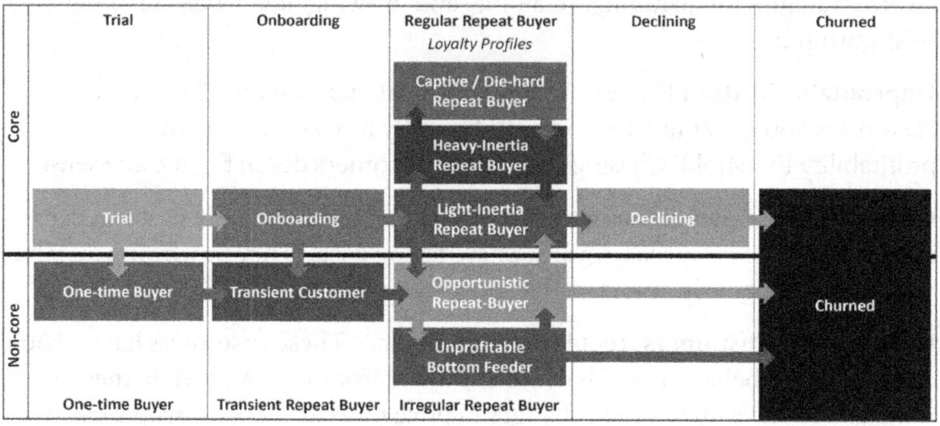


Using the customer lifecycle map above, you can see how every customer who has ever done business with you fits in only one box. And you can even trace the exact path the customer took to arrive at their current designation.

## Chapter Summary

In this chapter we've covered some foundational ways to categorize and better understand the composition of your customers, which should help provide context and visibility to pricing strategy opportunities.

"Customer loyalty" is usually a misnomer, as customers typically care much more about their own self-interest than devotion to any particular company. The **attributes of customer loyalty** are typically based on the customer's desire to minimize unnecessary costs and the ability to avoid costs by consolidating purchases with a small number of suppliers. These costs can include evaluation costs, transaction costs, fulfillment costs, and switching costs, and these costs tend to be amplified when customers need to make a greater number of repeat purchases. The more these types of cost are present, the more likely customers are to exhibit characteristics of "customer loyalty."

Most regular repeat buyers are **relationship buyers**, meaning they prefer to find fewer vendors that can provide many of the products and services they require at a fair price. Relationship buyers exhibit very different behaviors vs. product-level buyers or cart-level buyers. While both product-level buyers and cart-level buyers place a lot of importance on finding the lowest prices, relationship buyers assume prices will be in the competitive ballpark and place more importance on minimizing other costs of doing business, like minimizing evaluation, transaction, and fulfillment costs. Relationship buyers seldom switch due to the price of any individual product, as they are more concerned about the holistic aspects of the customer–vendor relationship.

Understanding the velocity of the business—the frequency with which most repeat customers make purchases—can inform the most appropriate customer lifecycle model and allow companies to appropriately interpret changes or gaps in customer purchase behavior.

There is a natural customer lifecycle model for every type of business, especially repeat-buyer businesses. The Universal Customer Lifecycle Model for Repeat-Purchase Businesses is a customer lifecycle model that can be adapted to most companies who sell to repeat-purchase customers. It includes core and non-core customer lifecycle stages.

**Core** customer lifecycle stages include **trial, onboarding, regular repeat buyer, declining,** and **churned**. **Non-core** customer lifecycle stages include **one-time buyer, transient repeat buyer,** and **irregular repeat buyer.** Using **customer lifecycle stages** as an initial customer segmentation can help you rapidly understand the composition of your customers and revenues, creating visibility on likely strategic growth opportunities. On top of these stages, improved granularity of repeat customers can be achieved by overlaying five basic customer loyalty profile stages, which include **unprofitable bottom feeders, opportunistic customers, light inertia repeat buyers, heavy inertia repeat buyers,** and **captive** or **die-hard customers**. Understanding how your existing customers fit among the different profiles will help you better focus your customer acquisition and retention strategies on customers who have a better potential for longer-term loyalty.

There are many different ways to segment your customers, and it's important to explore and evaluate what types of customer segmentation will allow you to find opportunities and create focused strategies to improve the value of your company via the **five sacred metrics of pricing success**. The standard customer lifecycle stages and standard loyalty profiles introduced in this chapter can create a very fast and meaningful way to segment your customers so that you can better understand the composition of your potential revenue-generation assets—your existing and future customer relationships.

CHAPTER 11

# Hypothesis-Based Pricing Transformation

**Case Parable 4: ChangeCo and New VP Pricing & Growth, Marta McLain**

## Chapter Overview

This chapter contains a case parable of Marta McClain, a newly hired VP of Pricing & Growth for ChangeCo, a $250 million provider of industrial-grade uniforms, safety vests, and construction apparel to manufacturing and construction companies. After recently reading ***Price for Growth***, she decides to implement some of the concepts of customer lifecycle progression to identify opportunities and create pricing incentive strategies to impact the value of the company. She convinced her bosses, both the CEO and CFO, to read the book, and they gave her their full support.

ChangeCo's revenue model was based on a monthly service fee, which included rental, cleaning, and repairing the products so their customers always had clean apparel in good condition and ready for use. Over the last three years, ChangeCo had an average annual net revenue growth rate of 11%. Approximately 20% of their revenues came from new customers each year, but their 9% customer churn constrained their annual net growth rate to only 11%. ChangeCo had impressive profit margins of 18%.

Marta quickly learned the history of how ChangeCo had attempted to acquire new customers. Their long-time approach was fairly simple:

- New prospects were offered a 50% off coupon for the first 30 days.

- They didn't have the concept of an "onboarding" period after the first 30 days.
- At the end of the 30 days, customers could get 20% off perpetually if they committed to use the product for the rest of the year. If they didn't stay for the full year, they were sent an invoice for the extra 20% discount they had received but hadn't earned.
- Customers who agreed to continue the service after the first year were allowed to keep their 20% discount perpetually.
- Customers who did not want to commit to long-term service simply paid list prices, which by themselves were pretty competitive in the market.

So, to sum up, customers were incentivized to try the service for 50% off list prices for 30 days, and as long as they were willing to commit to long-term use greater than one year, they got 20% off continued business. Irregular customers paid list prices.

After some analysis, Marta quickly set up a customer lifecycle model, so she could better track conversion metrics and identify opportunities to grow the value of the company.

She started with a report that showed average conversion rates shown in the table below:

**ChangeCo Historical Conversion Rates**

| From | To | Conversion Rate | Cumulative Rate |
|---|---|---|---|
| Lead | Trial | 20% | 20% |
| Trial | Onboarding | 40% | 8% |
| Onboarding | Regular | 80% | 6.4% |
| Regular | Declining | 12% | .77% |
| Declining | Churned | 75% | .58% |

Without doing any further analysis, Marta could see that the lead-to-trial conversion rates (20%) were significantly below industry averages (33%). She knew that was the first place they should focus.

## The First Pricing Strategy Experiment

She decided to do a 90-day promotion, where she would offer the first month for $1 (essentially a 100% discount) in order to improve the Lead-to-Trial conversion rate. Using best practices learned from the book, she made the change and observed the results, which were both good and bad. The lead-to-trial conversion rate had increased from 20% to 48%, a 140% increase! However, the conversion rate from **trial to onboarding** had simultaneously fallen from 40% to just 12%, which unfortunately decreased the overall lead-to-regular conversion rate from 6.4% to only 4.6%, shown in the table below.

**Initial Experiment Results for $1 First 30 Days Promotion**

| From | To | Original Conversion Rate | New Conversion Rate | Original Cumulative Rate | New Cumulative Rate |
|---|---|---|---|---|---|
| Lead | Trial | 20% | 48% | 20% | 48% |
| Trial | Onboarding | 40% | 12% | 8% | 5.8% |
| Onboarding | Regular | 80% | 80% | 6.4% | 4.6% |

Marta called her team together to have a brainstorming session on what might be happening and why. They hypothesized that they likely weren't getting conversions past trial because the difference between $1 and 80% of list price was too big of a jump—customers weren't getting used to paying real prices during the trial period vs. what they would be asked to regularly pay after the trial period. So, they decided to make a change to the promotion. Instead of $1 for the first month, they created a new promotion that would offer a 75% rebate after the first two months. Although not as big an incentive in the first month, it was actually a more significant incentive because it would last for two months instead of one. But by making it a rebate instead of a discount, the team felt that the customers would be more likely to get accustomed to paying regular prices for the service because the rebate wouldn't happen until after the first two months. They also felt that two months of the trial service would allow customers to start forming habits around the new service, so it would be more difficult to switch back to their old provider, as long as the service was good.

The new results were much better. Not only did they get the **lead-to-regular** conversion rates back to 6.4%, but they also almost doubled that benchmark, achieving 12.2%, shown in the table below:

**Revised Experiment Results for 75% Rebate Incentive**

| From | To | Original Conversion Rate | New Conversion Rate | Original Cumulative Rate | New Cumulative Rate |
|---|---|---|---|---|---|
| Lead | Trial | 20% | 38% | 20% | 38% |
| Trial | Onboarding | 40% | 40% | 8% | 15.2% |
| Onboarding | Regular | 80% | 80% | 6.4% | 12.2% |

After netting out the 9% revenue churn rate, the **net repeatable revenue growth rate** (NRRGR) grew from 11% to 29.1%, a 165% increase! This resulted in a theoretical company value that was 800% greater than when Marta had come on board, just over six months before! In just over six months, Marta had found a way to massively improve the value of the company.

## The Next Improvement Opportunity

After this first initial success, Marta turned her attention to the **Trial-to-Onboarding** conversion rate, hypothesizing that it could be improved by providing for an easier transition than the abrupt jump from 75% off during trial to only 20% off during onboarding. She hypothesized that a moderately declining rebate schedule that allowed the customers to make the transition over a period of 5 months would be more acceptable and easier for customers to stomach, so they created the rebate schedule shown in the table below:

**ChangeCo 75% Rebate with Declining Monthly Rebate Percentages**

| Timeframe | Rebate (paid at end of each timeframe) |
|---|---|
| Month 1 (trial) | 75% |
| Month 2 (onboarding) | 60% |
| Month 3 (onboarding) | 45% |
| Month 4 (onboarding) | 30% |
| Month 5 and beyond | 20% |

The new promotion system was implemented, and the results started to come in, largely improved as expected, as shown in the table below:

**Second Revised Experiment Results for 75% Declining Rebate**

| From | To | Original Conversion Rate | New Conversion Rate | Original Cumulative Rate | New Cumulative Rate |
|---|---|---|---|---|---|
| Lead | Trial | 20% | 36% | 20% | 36% |
| Trial | Onboarding | 40% | 56% | 8% | 20.2% |
| Onboarding | Regular | 80% | 84% | 6.4% | 16.9% |

Although the **lead-to-trial** conversion rates fell just a little, the **trial-to-onboarding** and **onboarding-to-regular** conversion rates were significantly higher. On an annualized basis, the new pricing incentive increased the new-customer revenue acquisition rate by 164.5% from the original 20% to 52.9%. Leaving the churn rate at 9%, the **net repeatable revenue growth rate** went up from the original 11% to 43.9%, a 299% increase. Plugging the new metrics into the company value calculator showed a new **theoretical company value** of 1500% more than when Marta had been hired, less than one year earlier.

## Marta's Next Improvement Focus: Churn

The the metrics showed that 75% of customers who entered the **declining** stage moved to the **churned** stage within just a couple of months. They decided to implement a program called "Operation Rescue," where they would reach out to any **regular-repeat-buyer** customer who went 45 days without making a purchase. This would entail interviewing the customer to find out the reason they had stopped purchasing, to see if it was service-failure related, competitive-price related, or something else, and then offer a special loyalty rebate of an additional 10% plus one free month to try to keep the customer.

For the next three months, ChangeCo executed Operation Rescue to see if they could materially reduce churn.

When the results came back, they learned something they didn't expect. For starters, 60% of the companies they contacted simply said they didn't need the service anymore—60% of the churn was unrecoverable. Next, they learned that 30% of the people they called had experienced a service failure of significant proportions. These service failures ranged from late deliveries to dirty/unkept clothing. What was more alarming was that most of them said they had been experiencing service failures for more than six months before they decided to change to another company. Marta was floored by this revelation, wondering if many of her other loyal customers might be experiencing the same thing.

Zero percent of the companies that experienced service failures would take ChangeCo's offer of one free month of service. That meant that price didn't matter at all, and the churned customers were evidently happy with their decision to leave.

Operation Rescue turned out to be an unexpected failure in terms of reducing the churn rate. However, ChangeCo was successful in capturing important information about their service quality, and they realized they needed to take action right away, which they did and which ultimately resulted in a 33% reduction in churn and a further increase in company value.

Later that year, the company did their IPO at an initial offering price that was 20x greater than when Marta first arrived.

## Chapter Summary

The ChangeCo case parable is full of lessons that can benefit any company considering a change in their pricing strategy to achieve a larger company value.

- Try to focus first on the area of the largest potential impact. Marta focused first on growth and conversion rates because they seemed to have the most room for improvement. Conversely, profits were already high, above industry averages. She knew (from her tools) that improvements to the net revenue growth rate would have a massive impact on the value of the company.
- Experiment in a way that doesn't negatively change existing customer expectations. Marta did experiments in trial and onboarding incentives fairy liberally because she knew that they could be done on a very short-term basis without changing existing customer price expectations. As a result, she was able to learn and then go back to "normal" if she wanted to.
- Use every initiative and experiment as a learning opportunity. Operation Rescue wasn't very valuable as a pricing strategy, but it turned out to be a critical learning opportunity, which probably saved the company from a very bad fate. As a result, they were able to act on what they learned and turn the situation around before it became an out-of-control problem.
- Pricing strategies can be much deeper and more complex than simply moving prices up and down. The pricing strategies employed by ChangeCo were more about incentives to change customer behavior than they were about converging on an "optimal" price level. ChangeCo needed to find ways to dislodge customer buying inertia and overcome switching costs in order to increase their ability to capture new customers. Traditional elasticity models would never have worked in this situation. But it was clear that buyers had various sensitivities to price in the context of what behavior they were willing to change. In Operation Rescue, churned customers were offered a free month of service, and none of them accepted that offer, even though they were paying higher prices to another vendor. You cannot describe this phenomenon in terms of elasticity and maximum willingness to pay. It was more about willingness to switch or willingness to try, and free wasn't good enough to get it done.

By dissecting pricing strategies into focused objectives to capture, retain, and grow customer relationships, instead of using a blunt-force technique to try to "optimize" profits, pricing strategies become more manageable and achievable. In this case parable, Marta showed us that focusing on high-impact opportunities combined with hypothesis-driven experimentation can result in massive changes to the ability of a company to generate larger growth which can exponentially affect the total sum of future profits—what really drives the value of a company.

PART 3

# Building Focused Pricing Strategies

*Where focus goes, energy flows.*

—Tony Robbins

CHAPTER 12

# The Concept of Elasticity vs. Growth

*We've done price elasticity studies, and the answer is always that we should raise prices. We don't do that, because we believe…that by keeping our prices very, very low, we earn trust with customers.*

—Jeff Bezos

## Chapter Overview

There are many misconceptions about price elasticity, even among people who have been in the industry for many years. This presents a problem. In order to construct growth-maximizing pricing strategies, it is critical to understand—without error or misconception—what elasticity is and how to apply its concepts.

Traditional elasticity-based price optimization models seek to predict the change in sales quantity for various potential price changes in order to calculate expected revenues and profits under each scenario. But elasticity-based optimization models are simply not appropriate for repeat-purchase businesses, where most purchase decisions are made at the relationship level, and where customer loyalty and switching costs are such significant factors in the risk of customer churn.

The question is not just whether a customer buys or not. The more important questions focus on how pricing strategies improve the way customers move through the customer lifecycle to become regular repeat buyers, and then what makes them continue.

The concept of elasticity has a role in how you should think about your pricing strategies, just not in the way it's usually talked about.

## What Is Elasticity?

When people in pricing use the term "elasticity," they are most likely referring to the conceptual relationship between pricing and sales volume. The notion that there is typically an inverse relationship between price and sales volume is perfectly fine. But beyond that, things seem to break down.

Many people in pricing seem to believe that there is an inherent numerical relationship between price and demand—akin to a natural law (like gravity), such that one could discover this constant numerical relationship, and thereby engineer a precise number of sales, just by moving to the appropriate price. This view of pricing and elasticity is problematic and typically leads to actions that do more harm than good.

In economics, the official term is Price Elasticity of Demand, and the formula to calculate it is:

$$\text{Elasticity} = \frac{\text{Percentage Change in Quantity Demanded}}{\text{Percentage Change in Price}}$$

What most people don't realize is that, based on the definition above, Elasticity is a backward-looking metric, not forward-looking. And contrary to the way most people use the term, there is no guarantee—or even an implication—that elasticity calculations at two different points in time would necessarily yield similar results. Elasticity is not a natural law. Changing a price doesn't automatically produce sales. Sales are produced when a customer's needs get big enough to cause a series of actions that result in something being sold.

Demand curves vastly oversimplify the process of buyers and sellers coming together to make economically beneficial trades. Yet, because of the simplicity of the picture, it is tempting to try to forecast demand curves for the purpose of making "optimized" pricing decisions. The illustration below shows how these "optimal" prices are determined. The straight line represents the demand (or elasticity) curve; the larger arc represents the achievable revenue curve; and the smaller arc represents the achievable profit curve, based on the demand curve and associated cost estimates. PR would be the "optimal" price to maximize revenues, and Pϖ would be the "optimal" price to maximize profits:

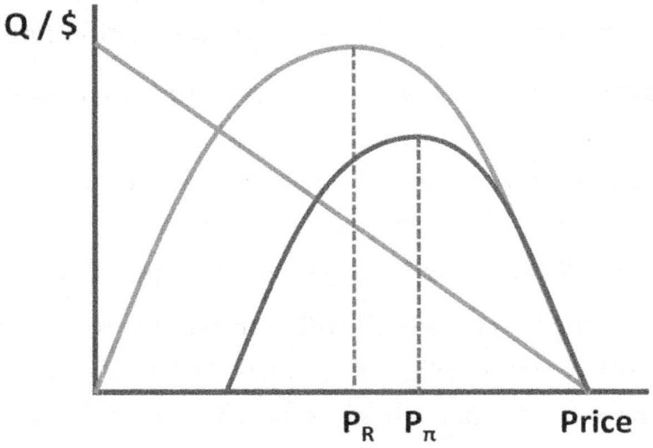


This is a nice, clean, and simple illustration of how elasticity-based pricing optimization systems work. The problem is simply that these models often overlook important complexities and biases in the process, such as the following:

- **The presumption that purchase decisions are driven only by price**. In reality, price is only one of literally hundreds of variables that affect customer purchase decisions, and most of the time, price is not the reason (deciding factor) somebody decides to buy or not.
- **The failure to consider the mechanical steps in the buying and selling process required to onboard new customers.** Typical elasticity models ignore all the steps in the buying process, except for the actual purchase of the product. For example, elasticity models don't consider that customers need to educate themselves on a product or service, or that they may need to be sold to.
- **The assumption perfect information.** Price elasticity models are based on the assumption that the customer has perfect information about not only the price of the product in question, but also all of the potential competing products.
- **The lack of consideration for real-world market friction, buyer inertia, and switching costs**. Often there are direct and indirect costs customers must bear to move from one supplier or product to another. Most of these models ignore the important factor of whether the customer is already purchasing the product or not.

The concept of price elasticity is real, but it's different than the way most people seem to understand it. The **five sacred metrics of pricing success** deal with new customer revenue growth, existing customer revenue growth, reduction of churn, expansion of repeatable profits, and reduction of risk regarding future profits. The most important elasticity questions should be based on how pricing strategies help to attract, retain, and grow customer relationships. For example:

- How does price affect a customer's willingness to learn about a product or service?
- How does price affect a customer's willingness to try out a product or service?
- How does price affect a customer's willingness to purchase a second time?
- How does price affect a customer's willingness to form a habit of buying a new product (instead of a competitor's product)?
- Once a customer has formed a habit of purchasing one particular product or service, what price incentive would cause them to try a competing product or service?

Additionally, how does a price or a price change impact a customer's belief that prices are fair? And what risks emerge when prices start to get out of line with "fair?"

These are particularly important questions because the long-term growth of the company depends on the ability to charge fair prices to the majority of the **regular repeat buyers**. If you miss on this, you will likely lose customers faster than you mean to. And you will hurt your net growth rates.

Even though a goal of elasticity modeling might be to determine the price at which customers stop buying, most studies show that approximately 70% of customer defections are due to service failures, not price. And price related reasons account for less than 20% of customer defections. If this is the case, how do you model customer defections without accounting for service failures?

Finally, anytime a company increases prices, it is generally advantageous to communicate with the customers what is happening and why it is necessary or justified. **Price communication** is a very important part of shaping customers' perception of fairness. And customers make decisions based on their perceptions, regardless of what is really happening with prices.

## Chapter Summary

Elasticity is an important concept, but it is often misunderstood. Sometimes it is used inappropriately to construct automated price optimization solutions, which often fail because they don't consider the inherent biases in the construction of the models. The important concepts of market friction, buyer inertia, and switching costs are often conspicuously missing in many of these attempted models, even though they have a massive impact on how customers make buying decisions.

The concept of elasticity is real and can be observed. But what is observed in history can seldom be turned around to engineer a target result just by changing the price. After all, a customer's decision to buy is a conglomeration of many different decisions, such as:

- a decision to pay attention
- a decision to learn
- a decision to try
- a decision to repeat
- a decision to substitute
- a decision to change behaviors to make buying easier

Good pricing strategists care about all of these decisions, and they are interested in how pricing, price strategies, or price incentives can lead customers to make positive decisions when the respective opportunities present themselves.

Studies consistently show that most customer defections are due to factors other than price. For that reason, churn models based solely on price should not be expected to yield much actionable insight.

Beyond initial incentives to buy a product for the first time, repeat-purchase customers generally like to settle into a new repeated buying behavior based on the assumption of fair and stable prices. Unfortunately, price changes can potentially upset the stability of customer buying patterns. It is important to communicate to customers a reasonable rationale for raising prices in order to avoid the risk of losing the customer's trust.

CHAPTER 13

# Objective-Driven Pricing Strategies

*Truth in science can be defined as the working hypothesis best suited to open the way to the next better one.*

—Konrad Lorenz

## Chapter Overview

The primary objective of pricing strategies should be to maximize the sum total of all future profits. The ability to accomplish this depends on ability to learn how to do it. There is no single one-size-fits-all approach to optimizing pricing strategies. Every company is different, and markets are always changing, so success depends on the speed at which companies can learn what works best for them at a given point in time.

The scientific method has long been an efficient methodology for learning and creating knowledge. The **scientific method** is a process for using ingenuity and creativity to analyze the situation, formulate questions, develop hypotheses, conduct tests, observe results, draw conclusions, and repeat the process. This process is illustrated in picture below:

**The Scientific Method**

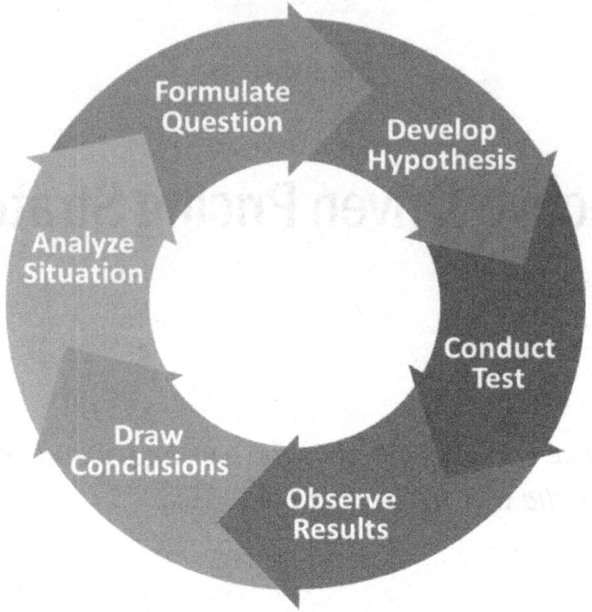


Pricing strategies that leverage the scientific method are called **hypothesis-based, objective-driven** pricing strategies.

## Hypothesis vs. Forecast

Too often people conflate mathematics as "science" and mathematical forecasts as the "science-based" approach to pricing. But in many ways, this is wrong. The true scientific method requires the use of a hypothesis which can be tested. Unfortunately, this is not how forecasts are typically viewed. Too often forecasts are treated like predictions of an inevitable future rather than a hypothesis to be used as a learning tool. The word "forecast" often promotes the mentality that the future is already defined, and you can't change it. All you can do is forecast it. And people sometimes drastically overweight the importance of a forecast, behaving as if it were an unavoidable fate. And when the forecast turns out to be wrong (as is frequently the case), people often blame the forecast for being wrong. And this allows people to separate themselves from the responsibility of the outcome. Because people often give too much weight to a forecast, they often tend to act helplessly instead of doing the things that would otherwise make them successful.

Conversely, people often discount the value of a hypothesis, but a hypothesis is an invitation to experiment and test. It offers a chance to either validate or reject, and in that sense, it is much more valuable than a forecast…because a forecast is not up for discussion.

Depending on which word we use, we may be inviting a different mindset and a different string of potential outcomes.

## Objective-Driven vs. Cause-and-Effect

There are two opposing approaches to determining optimal pricing strategies: the **cause-and-effect** approach and the **objective-driven** approach. In the **cause-and-effect** approach, the focus is on the "causes," and in the **objective-driven** approach the focus is on the "objective." To illustrate the difference in methodology, we use a scenario of a company considering a price increase for the purpose of improving profitability.

In the **cause-and-effect** approach, we start with the cause (raising prices) and try to estimate the effect (how much business we will lose). The question may seem to be focused and contained, but it is much more open-ended than it appears because there are many potential outcomes of raising prices which are typically ignored if not part of the focused question. For example:

- Per-unit profits will increase.
- Existing customers might become upset.
- Some customers may decide to leave.
- It may become more difficult to capture new customers.
- Competitors may change their pricing strategies.
- Employees and salespeople could become confused.
- Billing errors could happen if systems are not all updated correctly.
- Etc., etc.

The problem with this approach is that the company necessarily chooses to ignore some potential resultant effects for the sake of simplifying the problem. This approach might more appropriately be called **cause-and-some-of-the-effects** approach.

The **objective-driven approach** is different in that it starts with the end objective, and then works backwards. One may say, "I want to increase prices, and I don't want to lose any customers. But my main priority is to not lose customers." And so, the first step is to word the problem/objective statement such that it appropriately frames the priorities of the objective:

***How can I increase profits without losing any customers?***

While the cause-and-effect approach immediately presumed the causal action would be potential price increases, this problem statement does not restrict what the causal actions may be. Instead, the objective-driven approach might start making a list of all the potential ways the objective might be achieved by formulating several questions:

- What if I raised prices?
- What if I tried to increase profits by increasing the number of customers?
    - o What if I lowered prices to try to attract more customers?
    - o What if I hired more salespeople?
    - o What if I increased marketing investments?
    - o What if I tried to reduce customer churn by offering better service?
- What if I tried to increase profits by decreasing costs?
    - o What if I invested in people who could negotiate better costs?
    - o What if I committed to larger volumes with fewer vendors to get lower costs?
- What if I tried to increase profits by selling more to my existing customers?
    - o What if I found a way to resell somebody else's products?
    - o What if I developed new products to sell?
- Etc., etc.

The next step is to develop a **hypothesis**. Perhaps after reviewing all the potential causes, I form a belief that the quickest and easiest way to increase profits without losing any customers is to conduct a very small price increase. And so, I form the following hypothesis:

**Hypothesis:** I can raise prices by 1.5%, attributed to keeping up with general inflation, with no material loss of customers and without materially increasing the risk of future churn.

And in the spirit of learning and experimentation, that hypothesis can be tested, and quickly verified or rejected based on the results. In the objective-driven approach, I am more likely to use a hypothesis than a forecast due to the many different potential "causes" which may not have a ready-to-use forecast.

In the objective-driven approach, it is possible to develop a hypothesis, quickly test it, draw conclusions, and then revise the hypothesis and repeat the processes based on educated guesses about improving the results.

While the **cause-and-effect** (and forecast-assisted) approach can be insightful and interesting, the **objective-driven** (hypothesis-based) approach is generally advantageous for the following reasons:

- **Focus**: It keeps primary focus on the desired objective.
- **Engagement of creative thinking:** Because there is no pre-determined cause-and-effect forecasting model driving the process, decision-makers are free to explore multiple ways to accomplish the objective.
- **Provocation of learning and experimentation:** It naturally invites efficient ways to experiment and observe results to quickly learn.
- **Freedom from relying on forecasts:** Cause-and-effect decision-making depends on an accurate forecast to make decisions, but sometimes there is not sufficient data to produce an accurate forecast. You can test any hypothesis independently of sufficient data for forecasting.

Forecast-based decision systems typically suffer from data sparsity and/or data inaccuracy for a large portion of the decisions, the long tail that make up the smaller portion of the results. For this reason, an alternative approach for the long tail must always be conceived.

This is the fatal flaw of most forecast-based decision systems—they perform well in the highly populated segments, but they break down when they meet data sparsity.

People often get caught up in "bake offs" to compare "forecast accuracy," but most of the time it doesn't really matter, for the following reasons:

- Most pricing decisions are not permanent, and for the most part, they are easily reversed or corrected.
- The cost of getting the forecast more precise is usually much greater than the value of the benefit of the extra precision.
- Perfect forecasts can often be used as a crutch instead of inviting new hypotheses and testing to obtain new knowledge.

Many companies have foregone good strategy, instead letting "optimization solutions" define the default pricing strategy for short-term profit maximization. Good strategy is the process of constantly moving the company to a better position to achieve better profitability in the future. That means every move should help the company learn more, expand options, and enable a better "next move" in the future.

Risk mitigation and reversibility should be designed into pricing actions. This is the essence of good strategy.

Thinking in terms of **break-even outcomes** is an efficient way to make decisions (The opposite of break-even outcomes is scenario modeling, which can be very taxing and still not lead to a beneficial result).

There are three different types of break-even calculations.

- **Profit break-even**: What has to happen to keep the actions and results profit neutral over a 12-month period?
- **ROI (Return on Investment) break-even**: What outcomes are required to achieve a positive ROI over the life of the investment?
- **Company valuation-based break-even**: What outcomes are required to keep the company valuation neutral?

Break-even calculations are all about the incremental costs vs. the incremental benefits. Every pricing action has an incremental net cost. This can include foregone margins from existing or expected business when you lower a price or add a discount. It can also include the incremental costs to communicate the new pricing strategy to internal employees, resellers, and customers. It can include any additional administrative costs necessary to process any new pricing. You will need to decide what costs you will include in your break-even calculation.

To illustrate the different types of break-even calculations, we use an example of a company that is considering expanding their trial incentive discount from 10% to 30%, an incremental 20% discount.

The table below shows the 3 different break-even calculations:

| Break-Even Calculation | Incremental Cost (foregone profits) | Unitary Benefit (profit per incremental customer) | Break-Even Incremental Units (new customers) |
|---|---|---|---|
| Profit Break-Even | $10,000 | $450 | 22.2 → 23/mo |
| ROI Break-Even | $10,000 | $3,000 | 3.3 → 4 /mo |
| | Annualized Cost | Incremental company Valuation (per new incremental customer) | Break-Even Incremental Units (new customers) |
| Valuation-Based Break-Even | $120,000 | $66,600 | 1.8 → 2 /yr<br>Less than 1 per month |

To calculate the **profit break-even**, we divide the incremental cost ($10,000) by the profit expected in the next 12 months from each incremental customer ($450) to determine that we would need 22.2 additional customers to make this investment profit neutral over the next 12 months.

To calculate the **ROI break-even**, we divided the incremental cost ($10,000) by the expected lifetime incremental profit per new customer ($3,000) to determine that we need 3.3 new customers to make the investment break-even over the life of the investment.

To calculate the **company-valuation-based break-even**, we need to translate the numbers to annualized, so we divide the annual incremental cost of $120,000 by the amount of incremental company value each incremental customer would bring to the company (based on calculations in the company valuation calculator available on the website), which is $66,600, to determine that we need 1.8 incremental new customers each year to make the investment "accretive" to the value of the company.

Once you calculate the various break-even values, you can add your hypothesized outcome to help you make the decision on whether or not to move forward, as shown in the table below.

| Break-Even Calculation | Incremental Cost (foregone profits) | Unitary Benefit (per incremental customer) | Break-Even Units (new customers) | Hypothesized Incremental Units |
|---|---|---|---|---|
| Profit Break-Even | $10,000 | $450 | 22.2 → 23/mo | 100/mo |
| ROI Break-Even | $10,000 | $3,000 | 3.3 → 4 /mo | 100/mo |
| | Annualized Cost | Incremental Valuation (per new customer) | Break-Even Units (new customers) | Hypothesized Incremental Units |
| Valuation-Based Break-Even | $120,000 | $66,600 | 1.8 → 2 /yr<br><br>Less than 1 per month | 1200/yr |

If the hypothesized outcome is significantly larger than the break-even values, it can make for a very easy decision to move forward. Most pricing decisions are like this in that they don't require a great deal of precision in the hypothesized outcome. For the most part, once the break-even and hypothesized outcomes are calculated, the decision is a no-brainer.

The hypothesized outcome is important because it provides an initial expectation and a beneficial checkpoint in the learning process. Forcing yourself to put a best guess out there gives you the opportunity to test your gut instincts. By hypothesizing and experimenting, you are continuously learning and developing your creative problem-solving skills.

## Chapter Summary

Effective pricing strategies include a series of sequential steps to identify opportunities, hypothesize results, take controlled actions, observe results, draw conclusions, improve our position, and revise our strategy. In this chapter, we covered some important lessons on why objective-driven, hypothesis-based approaches to pricing strategies are so advantageous in comparison with traditional cause-and-effect, forecast-dependent pricing decisions, including the following:

- Forecasting systems encourage pricing decision-makers to place responsibility and blame on the forecast rather than their own actions, even though most people agree that forecasts will almost always be wrong.
- Using a hypothesis-based approach encourages creativity and the consideration of solutions that have never been tried, leading to accelerated learning and improvements.
- Objective-driven problem solving is more expansive than the cause-and-effect approach because it is not limited to focusing on only one presumed set of causal actions. Objective-driven approaches allow for creative and compound solutions that can easily be transformed into a single hypothesis that can be tested and revised as needed.
- Even though much attention has been devoted to forecasting systems over the last few decades, most of these pricing systems continue to suffer from data sparsity in many of the forecast entities. For this reason, the value of forecasting systems tends to be vastly overrated for pricing decision-making.
- In reality, most pricing decisions can be reversible, especially if mitigation and reversibility are designed into the pricing action.
- Advancements in pricing strategy are achieved when pricing actions are designed to produce both the hypothesized strategic benefit along with the potential to learn from the results of the pricing action.
- Thinking in terms of break-even outcomes allows for rapid evaluation of potential pricing actions with a built-in outcome hypothesis (which can always be used in the absence of another outcome hypothesis).

While there are clearly times that forecasting and automated decisions can improve processes and outcomes, most of the larger-impact pricing-strategy-driven outcomes are achieved by using creative thinking to take advantage of high-impact opportunities, using the scientific method to formulate questions, develop hypotheses, conduct experiments, measure results, and draw conclusions. Automated decision systems should be reserved for after the large strategic questions have largely been settled, and the organization is looking to fine tune. But for most companies, the fundamental pricing strategy questions are far from settled, so focus belongs there without the interference of forecast-based optimization systems.

CHAPTER 14

# Applying the 80/20 Principle

*Believe it or not, it's not only possible to accomplish more by doing less, it's mandatory.*

—Tim Ferris

## Chapter Overview

This chapter is about the process of finding and focusing on the relatively few inputs that will produce and improve the most outputs, often referred to as the 80/20 principle.

The 80/20 principle is observed in many aspects of business and life. It's not uncommon to see:

- 20% of customers make up 80% of revenues or profits
- 20% of the products generate 80% of the revenue
- 20% of the salespeople generate 80% of the sales
- 20% of the stores make up 80% of the profits

The 80/20 rule is actually quite easy to explain. It boils down to variability in outputs, combined with the tendency of more successful outcomes to be given the opportunity to repeat, along with the compounding nature of investments.

Looking at an illustration from baseball, 20% of the players generated 80% of the homeruns in the 2019 baseball season. On average the top 20% of players hit 22.8 homeruns each, while the bottom 80% who had "at bats" hit an average of 1.4 homeruns each. The best were 1500% percent more productive. But if you compare batting average, the top players hit an average of .277 while the bottom players hit an average of .193, only 43% better. But the reason they were 1500% more productive was because the top players were given 71 times more opportunities than the bottom players. And so, the smaller difference of 43% was amplified to 1500% because the best were given more opportunities.

This is why the 80/20 principle exists—because things that are even moderately more successful tend to get more focus, more opportunity, and more ability to experience compound growth.

- Perhaps 20% of the customers account for 80% of the revenues because everyone tends to focus on the customers with higher revenue potential.
- Perhaps 20% of the sales reps produce 80% of the sales because they are given the best leads and opportunities.
- Perhaps 20% of the products generate 80% of the sales because salespeople tend to sell the most popular products.

The main message of the 80/20 principle? Do more of what yields more and do less of what yields less.

If you look a level deeper, big differences in productivity and outcomes are attributable to valuable shortcuts that can massively improve outputs by doing things in a different (smarter) way, and it's often worth the time and effort, in an extremely lopsided way, to pause lower-yield efforts in order to find these smarter paths to success.

To illustrate, there is a story of a room with a million logs that must be chopped for the sum of $1 million. The first person works 14 hours a day for 3.3 years to chop all the logs, earning approximately $300k per year. However, the second person is told that the person before him chopped all the logs and got out in 90 days. So instead of working for 14 hours a day chopping logs, the second person spends only 2 hours per day chopping and 12 hours per day thinking and dreaming about better approaches and shortcuts to more efficiently chop the logs, which results in breakthroughs that allow them to finish the task in 2 months, as saving of 38 months of work.

This story highlights that the most valuable time is spent thinking of better solutions. Where the first person earned approximately $60 per hour chopping logs, the second person earned the equivalent of $1,379 per hour in the time used to think of a better solution. This highlights the value and importance of thinking time, a key tool to taking advantage of the 80/20 principle.

The 80/20 principle is all about finding shortcuts to productivity by "getting smarter." There are better solutions to be discovered, but they will never be discovered if we spend all of our time on lower-yield efforts. The universal history of progress shows that smarter solutions are there to be found in almost everything. Impactful ideas come because time is consciously reallocated from a known lower-yielding effort to the intent to find smarter solutions.

The 80/20 mentality is an extension of the growth mindset, which approaches problems with an openness to change and experimentation. When you expect a universe of infinite possibilities, new solutions will come to you.

In order to benefit from the possibilities of smarter solutions in a world full of 80/20 possibilities, the following four recommendations are advised:

1. **Create time and space for thinking.**
    a. Allocate high-value thinking time.
2. **Adopt the 80/20 mentality.**
    a. Everything is an opportunity to improve.
    b. Question everything.
    c. Make everything a learning experiment.
3. **Take actions to enable 80/20 benefits.**
    a. Simplify.
    b. Reallocate time.
    c. Reallocate investments.
4. **Analyze and measure.**
    a. Analyze to find opportunities.
    b. Measure the benefits of every action and change in strategy.

By going into the available data and looking for irregularities or the existence of specific 80/20 relationships, your thinking will expand, and you will start to see opportunities that you perhaps didn't see in the past.

Here are some bonus lessons, regarding the 80/20 rule in pricing.

**Learn to say no in a positive and liberating way:** Saying yes to higher-priority activities means saying no to lower-priority activities. Saying no is a requirement. The best way to say no is to affirmatively say what you will be spending your time on instead, e.g., "Given the value and importance of the work I am doing, I cannot afford the time to do anything else, including X."

**Block at least 30 minutes each day to just think and reflect**: It will help you ensure that all the rest of your time is spent on the highest-value use. Thinking makes you smarter. Asking yourself questions makes you smarter. Make sure giving yourself daily time to think is a high-priority activity. In your thinking time, ask yourself questions: In what ways could I make my time investments more valuable?

The 80/20 Principle is an extremely valuable tool if you use it to your advantage. It works by helping you find higher quality investments for your time, energy, and focus. When you find those higher quality investments, you can achieve extraordinary results by giving your efforts more opportunities to succeed. Apply this principle to your life, and let it guide you to make exponentially better pricing decisions.

## Chapter Summary

The 80/20 principle is often simply a way to marvel at disparity and variability in output. But the deeper-level benefits come only to those who get beneath the surface of the 80/20 principle, along with why it exists and what actions can be taken to leverage its influence in almost any aspect of pricing or life in general.

- The 80/20 principle exists anywhere there either is—or could be—disparity of output, indicating variable productivity.
- The obvious, no-brainer action is to prioritize investments based on their relative productivity; invest more in the inputs that result in greater-productivity outputs and less in the inputs that result in lesser outputs.
- The deeper-level lesson is to invest the time and focus to understand why the potential disparities exist in order to discover innovations beyond the obvious—to think of new and better approaches to achieve the same or more output.
- Doing more by doing less has two different meanings. First, do less of what produces relatively lower output. Second, spend more time imagining how to produce more output with relatively less effort.
- A few key practices together enable the types of game-changing innovations intended to be discoverable in the context of the 80/20 principle:
  - Allocate time for high-value thinking.
  - Adopt the 80/20 mentality: Opportunities are everywhere. Question everything. Make every major action a learning experiment.
  - Take actions to enable 80/20 benefits: Simplify. Reallocate time to high-yield activities. Reallocate other investments toward higher-yielding opportunities.
  - Consistently analyze and measure results to find opportunities and determine the effectiveness of strategies and actions.

- Saying yes to high-value activities means saying no to lower-value pursuits. Learn how to eliminate, offload, delegate, or outsource lower-value tasks in order to make room for efforts that will lead to much larger results—even if it's just thinking time. And learn how to say "no" in a positive way that maintains the growth mindset.
- Block a minimum of 30 minutes each day for a thinking session. Use this time to determine the most important questions to find the largest opportunities. And, like using one of your three wishes (in the genie story) to wish for more wishes, use your thinking time to figure out how to get more thinking time. Thinking is often the highest value activity you can spend your time on.

Using the 80/20 principle is an important prerequisite to improving the impact of investments in time, effort, attention, and any other scarce asset. Keep this in mind as you reflect on opportunities to use focused pricing strategies to make sizeable impacts to the value of your business.

CHAPTER 15

# Focused Pricing Strategies to Increase Customer Acquisition

*New customers are the best source of new business.*

—Frank Bettger

## Chapter Overview

For most companies, a small increase in the growth rate of new customer revenues translates to an exceptionally large increase in company value. Very few investments can yield higher returns than investments in company growth. Yet very few companies have dedicated pricing strategies focused on customer acquisition. This not only results in partially wasted sales and marketing investments, but it also limits the value of the company. If your company cares about growth, you should have pricing strategies specifically tailored to attract and onboard new customers. And those pricing strategies should be getting better over time.

This chapter covers key pricing strategies specifically tailored to increase customer acquisition. Customer acquisition is a core responsibility of many different functional groups in the organization. However, Pricing, combined with cross-functional participation, should be the primary owner of price-driven growth strategies. These strategies commonly include price incentives to motivate customers to learn about, try, and purchase products in repeat fashion.

Pricing strategies alone are not sufficient to drive maximum potential growth. In order to be successful, pricing strategies must be integrated with sales, marketing, and product strategies. Together, these coordinated growth efforts can produce the desired improvement across the core metrics of growth.

If a company can build a proven customer acquisition model that is both successful and sustainable, that company's potential growth is constrained only by its desired level of investment.

This chapter will cover three specific types of incentives to help you achieve improved new customer acquisition growth rates:

- **Learning incentives**: incentives for customers to **learn** about your products and services
- **Trial incentives**: incentives for customers to **try out** your products and services
- **Onboarding incentives**: incentives for customers to **purchase** your products and services on an ongoing basis in order to form a new habit of buying from you

These customer acquisition incentives typically include one or more of the following incentive forms:

- a **discount off the price** of a product or service realized at the time of purchase—this would also potentially include free products or services
- a **credit** with some monetary value, which can be used to purchase goods and services within some pre-defined boundaries or time periods
- a post-purchase **rebate** of money spent on a particular product or service
- a **money-back guarantee**, where a customer can recover some or all of the money spent with you if they are not completely satisfied with the purchased products or services (in some cases, the amount of the guarantee can be more than 100% of the purchase price)

Customer acquisition incentives attempt to either remove obstacles or compensate a customer for acting outside of their normal process in exchange for considering, learning about, trying, and/or purchasing products or services from you. These incentives can include both monetary and/or non-monetary features.

**Customer journey** models can be helpful for outlining the steps a customer must take to become a regular repeat customer. The customer journey model below is good because it illustrates a few different behaviors a price promotion could incentivize, and it maps nicely onto the standard universal customer lifecycle model in Chapter 10.

### Universal Customer Journey Model with Key Incentives

1. **Awareness →** *Learning Incentives*
2. **Learning →** *Trial Incentives*
3. **Trial →** *Onboarding Incentives*
4. **Onboarding**
5. **Regular Repeat Purchases (retention)**
6. **Advocacy (promoting to other customers)**

Marketing should be responsible for awareness, but part of this could and should be in the form of a learning incentive—something that entices a customer to learn more about your product and services, which puts it in the realm of pricing.

All incentives are defined by seven key dimensions:

1. **Magnitude**: the size of the incentive, typically in monetary terms
2. **Required Action**: what the customer has to do to receive the incentive
3. **Rationale**: the reason for the incentive—what outcome is desired
4. **Timing**: when the incentive is given and received by the customer
5. **Form**: defines whether the incentive is in the form of money, credits, free goods, services, warranty, refund, etc.
6. **Complexity**: how difficult the incentive is to understand or communicate
7. **Qualification**: refers to the limits of the incentive, which can be size, product scope, time limits, customer eligibility, etc.

As different strategies and structures are outlined, one should think about how each of these dimensions could be varied to improve the effectiveness of the incentive and make it more impactful for your business.

**Learning Incentives**: Although not typically at the top of the list for most pricing teams, it is both possible and sometimes advisable to incentivize customers to learn about your product through a price incentive, for example:

***Watch this YouTube video to learn how to get a free month's supply of coffee. The coupon code and instructions for redemption are found at the end of the video.***

The price incentive is the free month's supply of coffee. The intended behavior is for the customer to watch the YouTube video, which should help them learn about the virtues of the product. Thus, by making a free offer to them, the company is incentivizing a customer to teach themselves why they want to buy their product.

**Trial Incentives:** These are incentives for customers to experience the product without having to bear the full economic burden of a regular purchase. Measurements of the effectiveness of trial incentives should include both the number of leads that convert to trial and the number of leads that convert all the way to regular repeat customer. As we saw in the case parable with Marta and ChangeCo, it's possible to increase the trial conversion rate in such a way that the overall conversion rates actually get worse.

There are five common structures for trial incentives:

**Discounts:** Good when the customer already believes they will get benefit out of the product, and the price reduction tips the scales enough to induce the trial

**Free Product Samples:** Good when the customer doesn't know if they'll like the product or not, and they're not willing to take any monetary risk to find out (perhaps because they are already happy with whatever they are currently buying). Should be used when customers are likely to try product if it is free (and not waste it or leave it on the shelf).

**Post-Purchase Rebates:** Good when the customer needs to be "bribed" into a first purchase that requires a little extra effort, perhaps due to the need to set up accounts and payment information that will remove friction for future purchases.

**Free Spending Credits** (with monetary value): Good for getting a customer to shop and start to create habits and remove friction from future purchases. Also good for getting target customers to try out a whole customer relationship, although they can also be used to incentivize product-specific trials. Because they can be so expensive, they should be reserved for situations when there is a high likelihood of conversion after the customer samples the experience. Precision targeting can help with this.

**Money-Back Guarantees** (which could be up to 100% or more): Good economical way to incentivize trial for products and services customers are likely to really like once they try them, as they only cost money if the customer doesn't like the product or service. And for an even more compelling incentive, companies can offer a 200%-money-back guarantee, as long as the risks for abuse have been positively mitigated.

The type of incentive that will be most effective for you and your company will depend on how your target customers currently think about your product. If they are likely to desire the product without objection, then a small trial incentive or a money-back guarantee might be good enough to get them to try it. On the other hand, if your product or service is not already desired by your customers, then you may need a little more incentive to get them to move.

And you may need to first incentivize them to learn about the benefits of your product or service before you can jump to incentivizing trial. Refer back to this section when you start designing incentives for your company.

**Onboarding Incentives:** Onboarding incentives are those intended to make it easy for customers to buy from you during the onboarding period—the period of time it takes for customers to develop regular-repeat-buying inertia. The goal is that, by the end of the onboarding period, customers have already created habits and behaviors to solidify their buyer inertia and create some level of switching costs. For this reason, it's important to design an incentive that reinforces the behavior and experience of regular buying, so the behavior will continue after the incentive has expired. And **post-purchase rebates or credits** are generally preferred because they are somewhat disconnected from the actual purchase experience.

Another popular approach to onboarding incentives is a declining rebate, where the larger discounts are offered up front when the relationship is young, and then, over time, as more buying inertia is being created, the discount slowly gets smaller, until it ultimately fades into the background.

Another approach is to structure the incentive such that the customer gets the rebate after a feedback session regarding your customer service. This gives your company one more touchpoint during which the customer's temperature can be taken to gauge the likelihood of future purchases after the incentive has expired, and mitigating action can be taken if necessary.

It's important to make sure your incentives don't inadvertently set erroneous long-term price expectations. For this reason, it's important to communicate that any incentive price is both short term in duration and different from regular fair prices, and use the following tips:

1. Label the incentive as a **trial** incentive (or something appropriately similar), so the customer understands that the purpose is to get them to try the product, and it is not meant to be a long-term price inducement.
2. Make it clear that the incentive is available for a limited time or limited use, such as "valid only for first 30 days of purchases" so the customer has a clear expectation that the promotional price will expire.
3. Give the customer visibility into what the regular price will be after the incentive.
4. Limit the duration of the incentive to only what is needed to achieve the stated effect. Generally, 30–90 days should be sufficient.

5. If you ever run into a situation where you believe a long-duration incentive is required, it will likely be better to charge the customer the regular price, and then give the incentive in the form of a rebate or free products, or some other lump sum approach, so the customer will be accustomed to paying the regular, fair price after the incentive has expired.

Avoid making existing customers angry with discounts they can't have. If existing customers see you handing out lower prices to new customers, you should expect that they will feel entitled to the same lower prices, especially if they are long-time, loyal customers. Here are a few tips to avoid this awkward situation:

1. Never offer new customers long-term pricing that is not offered to existing customers. Typically, if existing customers see a very short-term or a limited scope promotion, they are less likely to be affected by it.
2. Always state the objective of the incentive in order to make it clear to existing customers that the incentive is not applicable to them. For example: ***Register your business account on our online store and get a $100 credit toward your first purchases.***
3. Try to structure and describe the incentive such that it seems reasonable; so that it seems like a fair exchange for the prospective customer's burden; and so it doesn't sound discriminatory to existing customers.

### Justifying the Cost of Growth

Remember to consider investments using a break-even mentality and using all three break-even values, not just the one-year-profit-break-even value. The reality is most companies massively underinvest in their own growth, and as a result, they make themselves vulnerable to competitors that decide to make growth a priority. The five sacred metrics of pricing success and the company valuation calculator will give you the tools you need to make the case to justify the necessary investments for growth.

## Chapter Summary

In summary, new customer acquisition must be among the most important objectives of growth-focused companies. But the pricing strategies to achieve new customer growth are more complex than just providing a lower price. Most new-customer-acquisition-based pricing strategies are defined in the form of incentives. It is important that these incentives be seen as an integral part of a standard pricing schema that is fair, rational, and transparent. All incentives are defined and constrained by seven dimensions: **magnitude, required action, rationale, timing, form, complexity,** and **qualification**.

Focused pricing strategies to increase new customer acquisition include three main categories: (1) learning incentives, (2) trial incentives, and (3) onboarding incentives.

- **Learning incentives** are useful for helping your customers learn about the benefits of your products and services that may increase their desire to try or to purchase them. An example of a learning incentive might be a credit or discount that becomes available after watching an online video explaining the benefits of buying from your company.
- **Trial incentives** are useful for getting prospective customers to sample the experience of buying from you and using your products. They can come in the form of discounts, rebates, spending credits, or money-back guarantees of 100% or more. Their main purpose is to reduce the prospective customers' risk and/or the inconvenience associated with trying a product they don't know whether they will like or not.
- **Onboarding incentives** are meant to make it easy for a customer to develop recurring purchase habits with you and to make it difficult for them to switch to another provider that comes along in the future. The important aspect of onboarding incentives is to separate the incentive from the regular purchase experience in order to condition the customer to the experience they will receive when the incentive period is complete.

It is critically important to ensure that your targeted pricing incentives are seen for what they are—short-term incentives to try and onboard—in order to prevent accidentally setting the wrong customer expectation for long-term, regular prices. The incentives should last no longer than necessary (rarely longer than 90 days) to accomplish their intended objective.

It is also important to make sure that NEW-customer acquisition incentives don't negatively impact the attitudes of existing customers. This may take a little extra work, but it's worth the effort to maintain good customer relationships.

When considering the cost, benefits, and ROI of acquisition incentives, it's important to look at the real opportunity cost, which is the amount of increase in the value of the company that would be foregone by not investing sufficiently in new customer acquisition incentives. Accounting and Finance departments are famous for crushing investments that would otherwise make the company a Star.

Focused pricing strategies to increase the acquisition of new customers may be the most important strategies in terms of their potential impact on overall company growth and therefore the overall valuation of the company.

CHAPTER 16

# Focused Pricing Strategies to Increase Existing Customer Revenues

*It is generally agreed that is costs 5 to 10 times more to bring on a new customer versus keeping and developing an existing one.*

—Julian Patel

## Chapter Overview

This chapter is about pricing strategies and incentives to increase the growth rate of revenues to existing customers, the second sacred pricing metric. Increased sales to existing customers typically fall into one of two categories: (1) the organic growth of existing customer needs, and (2) selling existing customers products they're not currently buying from you. Both are important to understand and recognize. Depending on the industry, organic customer revenue growth can easily be as high as 2%–5% per year, and in some cases, 10% or more. The beauty of this source of customer growth is that it usually requires no additional price incentives. For this group, the most important price-related practice is keeping customer relationships strong through fair and transparent pricing.

In order to accomplish the objective of selling more to existing customers, pricing strategies must incentivize customers to act in a slightly different way. In this case, you want customers to buy additional products that they are not currently buying from you. Presumably, they're already buying those products from another vendor. Maybe the price–value equation with the other vendor is more attractive. Maybe it's just a result of buying inertia created over a long period of time. New pricing incentives must be compelling enough to disrupt their existing behavior and get them to see a better overall value proposition by purchasing those products from you.

There are five different types of incentives you can use, either individually or in combination with another incentive, to try to increase sales to existing customers:

1. **Overall-purchase-volume incentives**: Incentivizing customers to buy more of anything, typically in the form of rebates or earned discount levels.
2. **Product-specific purchase-volume incentives**: Incentivizing customers to buy specific products. Good for situations where the opportunity is with a specific product line, perhaps after an acquisition or new product introduction.
3. **Portfolio-breadth incentives**: Incentivizing customers to buy more categories of products from you, perhaps a rebate percentage that grows depending on how many categories they buy from you.
4. **Purchase-volume growth incentives**: Incentivizing customers grow their rate of increased purchases. This is a good way to incentivize new customers without irritating existing customers, although this is typically more effective when combined with another incentive like an overall purchase volume incentive.
5. **First-spend incentives** (on specific products or categories): Incentivizing customers to buy products and services they haven't bought before. This is good for getting customers to start the process of creating buyer inertia by buying a new product from you.

It is imperative that customer relationships are treated with extreme care. This means always adhering to a **standard pricing and discount schema** with objective eligibility criteria that customers can trust.

As you put together your incentive structures to try to increase revenues from existing customers, it's helpful to follow ten key guidelines.

1. **Simple and straightforward:** Make sure your incentives are easy to communicate and easy to understand. Avoid complexity, especially unnecessary complexity.
2. **Connect incentives to controllable behavior:** Customers need to be able to see a connection between the reward and behavior they can control. Poorly set up incentive programs can be demotivating and even make customers angry.

3. **Make new or experimental incentive programs limited-time opportunities,** so you can retract and/or alter them if they're not yielding desired results.
4. **Focus on just one or two incentives at a time:** Too many incentives are difficult to keep track of and can actually hurt customer motivation.
5. **Test different incentive values:** Start with an initial hypothesis and see how it works. If it's not working the way you expected, try something else. Always be learning.
6. **Communicate frequently and reinforce communication:** Incentives work only if they are present and understood in the minds of your customer decision-makers. Reinforce your communication with reminders on invoices, rebate statements, and any other regular communication vehicles.
7. **Measure and simplify:** If your incentives are not producing desired results, get rid of them. In the world of pricing, incentives, and customer attention, less is more. Fewer incentives will be more powerful than many incentives.
8. **Make sure everything seems fair and transparent:** You never want a customer to feel slighted because they didn't know about a rebate opportunity.
9. **Keep track of overlapping incentives.** Don't let overlapping incentives kill your profitability or confuse your customers. Keep overlapping incentives to a minimum.
10. **Avoid frequent incentive changes and contradictory incentives:** Avoid changing incentives every week or every month. Give them time to play out. Give your customers time to process them and take the necessary time to act.

## Chapter Summary

Selling more to existing customers can be a sustainable way to grow revenues at a repeatable rate, thereby growing the value of your company.

There are two main drivers of revenue growth from existing customers: (1) the organic growth of existing customer needs, and (2) selling existing customers products they're not currently buying from you.

As far as pricing is concerned, there is really only one growth scenario that seems to be primarily driven by price—cross-selling additional products that the customer is not currently purchasing from you.

Pricing incentives can be used to capture additional sales from existing customers, but they must be compelling enough to disrupt the existing buyer inertia your customers have developed with your competitors. Sometimes the trial and onboarding incentives discussed in the previous chapter are more appropriate than the purchase-volume incentives covered in this chapter. Often, both types of incentives can effectively be used together to dislodge inertia and grow the volume of purchases from your company.

There are five different types of pricing incentives that can be used to incentivize existing customers to purchase more from your company:

1. Overall-purchase-volume incentives
2. Product-specific purchase-volume incentives
3. Portfolio-breadth incentives
4. Purchase-volume growth incentives
5. First-spend incentives (on specific product or category)

Each of these incentive structures have their own respective pros and cons, which make them more or less appropriate for different situations. Some of them can be overlaid on top of other incentives to create a comprehensive, long-term, pricing incentive system that can effectively deliver on your pricing strategy.

You must use your knowledge of these incentives, combined with the specific situation of your business, to hypothesize and experiment to determine the best combination of incentives to drive maximum growth for your business.

Effective incentive programs for existing customers should follow ten key guidelines:

1. Keep incentives simple and straightforward.
2. Ensure incentives are connected to controllable behavior.
3. Default to short-term, limited-time opportunities.
4. Focus on just one or two incentives at a time.
5. Test different incentive values to find what works best.
6. Communicate frequently and reinforce communication.
7. Measure and simplify by removing ineffective incentives.
8. Make sure everything seems fair and transparent.
9. Don't let overlapping incentives hurt profitability or confuse customers.
10. Avoid frequent changes to incentives and the presence of contradictory incentives.

The key to maintaining and growing existing customer relationships is to consistently deliver good service combined with fair prices and effective long-term, volume-based discount structures that never undermine customer satisfaction. In all cases, the strength of the customer relationship should be the highest priority, even higher than gaining additional revenues. This means never breaching the implied commitment to offer fair and standardized prices and discounts to all customers who objectively qualify.

CHAPTER 17

# Focused Pricing Strategies to Reduce Customer Churn

*The key is to set realistic customer expectations, and then not to just meet them, but to exceed them— preferably in unexpected and helpful ways.*

—Richard Branson

## Chapter Overview

This chapter is about pricing strategies to reduce customer churn, the third sacred pricing metric. Unfortunately, there is no single silver bullet. High value customer relationships require a culture of care and a total company commitment to meeting customer expectations—or, ideally, exceeding them. High levels of customer churn can cripple net growth rates.

Not all customer churn is preventable, so this chapter focuses on preventable churn. In order to do this, it important to understand what is causing preventable churn.

Studies show that approximately two thirds of customer churn is due to service failures and/or poor handling of service failures. Only about 20% of churn is typically attributable to price. So, at the very least, pricing people should have awareness of service failures, so they can avoid increasing prices at the wrong time, as they might aggravate an already bad situation.

Unfortunately, in the context of repeat purchases, where buyer inertia and switching costs are big impediments to change, when a customer finally decides to leave, it is usually too late to change their mind. If the incumbent vendor doesn't see this coming until after the customer has moved, the customer has already incurred the majority of the switching costs. The ship has sailed. Whatever was keeping the customer in the relationship before, despite the service failures or poor customer experience, is now gone.

Pricing chasing (lowering a price to try to keep a customer who has left due to a lower price) and rescue pricing (offering a low price to win back a customer who has left due to a service failure) almost never work and usually miss the mark.

The best time to mitigate customer churn is before it happens.

This is why it's so valuable to have an early warning system to alert companies to situations that could result in churn before the customer crosses the threshold of "too late."

But how can pricing strategies assist in creating an early warning system? One way is to use a pricing incentive to entice customers to participate in customer satisfaction surveys. This is typically not thought of when considering pricing strategies to reduce churn, but it may be the most effective way to actually prevent it.

Beyond that, we have incentives that really serve as "bribes" to keep customers loyal, but these incentives are really just band-aids meant to make up for questionable service and value proposition. Since it's nearly impossible to provide blemish free service at all times, we will consider them as well.

And so, for churn prevention, there are four main pricing strategies or incentives that should be considered:

1. **Customer satisfaction survey incentives**: Where customers are offered a rebate or discount in exchange for their participation in regular (e.g., quarterly) customer satisfaction surveys. This can be an effective way to install an early warning system to detect customer dissatisfaction before they get to the point of switching to another provider.
2. **Commitment discounts**: These are discounts offered to customers in exchange for a promise or "commitment" to source a certain percentage of their relevant products and services from the company. This incentive system doesn't really have any teeth, but it is better than getting nothing back for an offered discount, and it can serve as an objective rationale for offering discounts that is easy for customers to accept.
3. **Earned discounts or rewards**: These are discounts that are calculated based on actual purchases, so as customers do more business, they actually earn bigger discounts. The problem with this type of incentive is that it offers little

defense for competitors that come in with a lower price. Like commitment discounts, this type of discount can make the customer slightly more psychologically committed to buying from you.

4. **Deferred-reward loyalty incentive systems**: These are proven to be the most effective loyalty incentive systems because they actually hold the customer "hostage" during a deferral period (typically 3-12 months), where they have to keep buying from you in order for their rewards to vest. While they are waiting and spending money with you, they are building up the next big reward that will hold them "hostage" during the next vesting period. I use the word "hostage" somewhat jokingly, but it illustrates what these incentive systems are really doing. And just because these types of incentive systems have proven to be effective doesn't mean they always make customers happy. When the incentive system is powerful enough to really be effective, that means customers feel they have to do business with you even if they don't think you provide the best product or service value proposition. And this may not be the best place to be.

A word of caution on deferred incentives (and really any incentive program that effectively controls or influences customer behavior): Don't rely on an effective loyalty incentive program to make up for bad service or poor pricing. Sometimes incentive programs can become so powerful that they actually mask a deteriorating customer experience and value proposition. If companies become complacent, they can unwittingly become overconfident about the value they are providing to their customers and fail to recognize or remedy a declining customer experience or pricing misalignment. All the while, customers may feel like they are trapped in a bad vendor relationship, wading through poor service or poor prices just because the reward at the end is too big to ignore. This eventually ends with the customer actively looking for a way out. When it finally gets bad enough for customers to leave, it can be nearly impossible to get them back. Once the incentive is gone, there is no longer a reason to continue the relationship.

To prevent this type of situation, companies need to have a good way to gather information on customer satisfaction levels. The best incentives will provide customers with incremental benefit on top of an already great customer value proposition. Companies would often do better to focus on minimizing and appropriately addressing service failures, rather than implementing loyalty incentives.

That said, a well-designed loyalty incentive can almost always help to provide another layer of protection against customer churn. And loyalty incentives will generally perform better if they adhere to the following eight guidelines:

1. The magnitude of the incentive needs to be significant enough to affect the customer's behavior.
2. The incentive will work better if the customer has to do something to earn it. This makes it feel personal and deserved.
3. It should be simple enough to be understood and present in the minds of customers as they make purchase decisions.
4. Customers should always be able to easily see how they're doing on meeting the incentive criteria and what the impact of the incentive is likely to be.
5. Deferred incentives tend to outperform immediate incentives because they create a situation where there is always significant benefit down the road, as long as the customer keeps buying.
6. Incentives should never create a situation where a customer's employee is tempted to behave unethically.
7. The loyalty incentive should never replace good service and compelling value. It should be an additional benefit.
8. Loyalty incentives should always be measured and monitored to evaluate their effectiveness on a cost–benefit basis. Simple is better, and less is more. When in doubt, cut it out.

Loyalty incentives can be an effective way to reduce churn when they are well designed and well communicated to the customer base. But they should never be the whole answer. Most importantly, loyalty incentives should be integrated into the overall pricing strategy for the whole business.

## Chapter Summary

Customer churn happens in all repeat-purchase businesses. Some is preventable, and some is not. Companies should do research to understand why customers leave and what portion of their churn is preventable, so action can be taken if desired.

Studies show that, on average, only about 20% of preventable churn is due to price. The other 80% is due to other factors, such as service failures, that cause dissatisfaction in the relationship. This is important to understand because a large portion of service failures are preventable. While pricing is typically not responsible for operational service failures, an ill-timed price increase can sometimes push high-risk customers over the edge. For this reason, it is critical that Pricing has the pulse of the current levels of customer satisfaction and the company's history with service failures.

Once otherwise loyal customers have decided to switch, it's usually too late to try to mitigate. At that point they've decided that it is more costly to continue buying from you than to bear all the switching costs and change to another vendor. **Rescue pricing** almost never works. The one exception is when customers have no better place to go. Even then, rescuing the customer requires more than just a good price. Price is almost never the reason customers leave when they have no other place to go. Rescuing an angry customer will typically require personal attention, combined with a genuine effort to mitigate the service failures that are causing the customer's dissatisfaction.

When customers leave due to lower prices offered by the competition, **price chasing**—offering a lower price to try to win back the customer—is almost never a fruitful effort. Disloyal customers will always chase lower prices, and their business will have little impact on long-term company valuation.

On the other hand, when an otherwise loyal customer decides to stop buying from you due to a lower competitive price offer, that generally means something big is going on because loyal customers seldom leave due to price. Whatever it is, it must be understood and addressed to ensure that you don't have a strategic vulnerability with your other loyal customers.

Simply put, an ounce of prevention is worth a pound of cure. There are four different types of pricing strategies that can help prevent customer churn:

1. **Survey participation discounts:** Pricing incentives for customers to participate in regular customer satisfaction surveys can serve as an early warning system for simmering problems that could later turn into churn.
2. **Commitment discounts** give customers financial incentives to commit to giving the company a certain amount of their purchases. While they can make the customer feel like they are receiving special treatment, they typically don't have enough teeth to keep customers from moving to a lower-priced vendor. But they can be a part of a total solution.
3. **Earned discounts or rewards** require customers to do a certain amount of business before they get the reward. Even though these programs are more compelling than commitment discounts, their potency can vary as customers get closer to or further away from the next reward.
4. **Deferred reward loyalty programs** are systems of reward that have incentives that customers earn but are deferred in their vesting for some predetermined vesting period. This helps to keep the customer loyal and simultaneously earning their next reward while they wait for the previous reward to vest. While these are inherently more complex and more difficult

to explain and understand, they can be among the most powerful incentives when well designed and successfully implemented.

While loyalty discounts and rewards programs can be effective in preventing customer churn, it's important that they are built on top of the foundation of solid customer experiences and relationships. Too often these programs turn into bribery to make up for an otherwise poor customer experience, and companies end up paying more than necessary to keep customers coming back. Worst of all, this can cause customers to feel angst about the relationship—having to put up with a poor experience in order to receive the rewards that have built up.

In the end, there are many ways to reduce churn through pricing. But the most important way is to ensure that your pricing is fair, transparent, rational, and easy to understand. This will build trust and make it easy for your company to be the default choice for your customers' future purchases.

CHAPTER 18

# Focused Pricing Strategies to Expand Margins

*Look for companies with high profit margins.*

—Warren Buffet

## Chapter Overview

This chapter deals with pricing strategies to expand margins through price increases. Although price increases can add risk to customer relationships and are, therefore, not sustainable long-term mechanisms to grow profits, there are definitely times when price increases for margin expansion are appropriate and acceptable. This is usually the case when market costs and prices are increasing or when company margins are unacceptably low. The company value calculator is the best way to identify and confirm the appropriate opportunities to expand margins through price increases. And this will be the case as profit margins get closer to zero percent. This is when profit increases have the most leverage.

In considering price increases, it is critical to understand the lifecycle stage each customer is in because price increases are more likely to be accepted by customers who have already developed entrenched buyer inertia.

This chapter covers three categories of margin expansion:

- **Reducing Costs**
- **Removing Discounts**
- **Raising Prices**

Margin expansion strategies are different from growth strategies in that they are generally implemented as one-time corrections, not sustainable or repeatable sources of profit growth. Furthermore, margin expansion can add significant risk to existing growth and churn-prevention efforts if it pushes beyond what is considered fair and competitive in the marketplace.

## Reducing Costs

Although the primary focus of this book and chapter is about pricing strategies, cost reduction opportunities should not be ignored. Most companies can find opportunities to either buy better or reduce costs through greater efficiency. Here are some possible suggestions to reduce costs:

- Negotiate lower prices with existing vendors
- Conduct a Request for Proposal (RFP) from several companies
- Dual source your supply
- Ask for alternative payment terms

Getting lower costs is a way to increase margins without putting your customer relationships or growth rates at risk.

## Removing Discounts

While there are clear situations when discounts should be removed (discussed below), you should never remove a discount when it would be a breach of ethics or when it would cause a profitable customer to stop doing business with you. **Growth** and **ethics** should both be at the forefront of your mind anytime you are contemplating whether or not to take something away from your customers. With this in mind, here are three situations where discounts should probably be removed:

1. Customers are unprofitable
2. The discount is based on criteria the customer doesn't meet
3. The reason for the discount has expired

In order to reduce potential negative effects of removing discounts, it's important to effectively communicate with the customer why the discount is being removed while simultaneously communicating commitment to fair and ethical customer interactions. The following elements will aid in this communication:

- Focus on the company's commitment to offer fair and transparent pricing.

- Remind the customer of how they benefit from fair and transparent pricing practices—primarily that they will never have to worry about overpaying.
- Explain how the change in discount is in line with the company's fair pricing commitment and, specifically, why it is justified.
- Talk about why the new price situation is still a good value for the customer.

While good price communication is sometimes a hassle, it can make a big difference in keeping customers in a good place and minimizing disruption to their existing buying inertia.

## Raising Prices

Sometimes, companies simply must raise prices to get profit margins in the right range. The most critical element of raising prices is to successfully communicate to the customer why the price change is justified, fair, and necessary. This requires effective **price communication**.

Effective price communication depends on the type and magnitude of the price increase. There are three main "flavors" of price increases, each with unique communication challenges:

1. **A general "across the board" price increase**: This is where a company undertakes a general price increase, raising the prices of most or all products and services, typically in response to **rising costs** or **a new business year**.
2. **A select price increase**: This is where a company raises the prices of specific products, typically in response to either a cost increase or a reassessment of the market value of a product.
3. **A mix of price increases with a few price decreases**: This is where a company seeks to better align margins or market prices with movements in the market by using a mix of price increases and price decreases. Although there are plausible scenarios where this strategy makes sense, as a default this should be avoided. Companies seldom get the same credit for lowering prices as the penalty they get for raising them. Furthermore, there is no guarantee that the customers who buy the products whose prices are being raised will also buy the products whose prices are being lowered, so some customers may see it only as a price increase.

There are four main potentially justifiable reasons for raising prices. The first two are typically more accepted by customers. The second two are typically not very well accepted by customers. Ultimately, the success of any price increase depends on your ability to effectively communicate the justifiable rationale to your customers.:

1. **Passing on a cost increase**: The most acceptable rationale for raising prices is to pass on a cost increase. Most customers don't expect vendors to unreasonably absorb cost increases from their vendors.
2. **Generally keeping up with inflation**: Many companies take a mild price increase at the end of the year under the general rationale that inflation is broadly increasing the cost of living, and therefore price increases are acceptable to keep pace with overall price levels.
3. **The product has been previously underpriced leading to scarcity of supply in the market and an adjustment is needed**: Most customers do not like this rationale, and they are more likely to resist and challenge it. CAUTION: NEVER USE SCARCITY AS A JUSTIFICATION FOR PRICE GOUGING. PRICE GOUGING IS NEVER OKAY.
4. **The value of the product has increased:** Sometimes companies increase prices due to the addition of incremental features and benefits. This is another one that customers don't typically like very much. How Much Is Too Much?

Although it will depend on the specific situation and industry, the following table outlines general rules of thumb regarding the riskiness and acceptance of different price increase magnitudes:

**Price Increase Range vs. Risk Table**

| Price Increase Range | Noticeability and Impact | Risk Level |
|---|---|---|
| 0–1% | Negligible impact. Customers won't take much notice. | Very Low |
| 1–2% | Small, but potentially noticeable. Most customers won't object. | Low |
| 2–5% | Questionable. Will raise eyebrows. Will need to be justified by acceptable rationale. Might want to look at competitive prices again. | Medium-Low |
| 5–7% | Significant. Likely to send customer looking at alternatives. | Medium-High |
| 7–10% | Warning: probably too high for the customer to accept without seeing corroborating evidence in the market that all prices are going up. Customer may conclude that you are attempting a profit grab. Either way, the relationship should be re-evaluated | High |
| 10–15%+ | Red Alert: If this is not happening across the whole market, the customer has reason to look for another vendor. | Very High |

It is recommended that you create a table like this for your own industry and customers based on your own company experience. It can be extremely helpful for planning price changes when necessary.

Keep in mind that every time you raise a price, you add risk to the customer relationship, especially if the particular product is already priced relatively high compared to alternatives in the market. Most price increases should be seen as one-time corrective actions.

**Low-Risk Price Increases:** Low risk price increases can be accomplished by concentrating those increases into lower risk products, as defined by the following criteria:

- products that are currently low price or low margin relative to the rest of the market
- products that are seldom purchased
- products that are not easily substitutable or "commodity" in nature
- products that haven't had a price increase for a long time
- products that are NOT high-visibility or image products (an image product is a product where customers already have an expectation of what the price should be, and from which customers form opinions of how the company prices ALL their products)

There are several tools that can help you identify good product candidates for low-risk price increases, depending on what data you have available.

**Segmented price targeting** is a term used to focus price increases on customers who are paying relatively low prices compared to the rest of their "segment." But as I've stated repeatedly in this book, customer-specific pricing typically goes against the principles of fair and transparent pricing, and you'll probably get better results moving to a standardized pricing.

## Chapter Summary

While margin expansion is rarely a repeatable source of profit growth, there are times when it should be a high-priority strategy. Usually, it should be approached as a one-time, corrective action rather than an ongoing effort. However, sometimes regular price increases are necessary in order to maintain existing margins, especially in markets that experience constantly increasing costs.

Margin expansion typically becomes important when margins have become unacceptably small or when growth strategies have stopped yielding sufficient results. Margin expansion strategies can include cost reduction or net price increases. And net price increases can be achieved by either raising list prices or removing discounts that are no longer valid. Either way, companies should be careful not to do anything that would risk damaging customer relationships. Giving undeserved discounts to one customer can damage relationships with other customers, as it erodes the perceived fairness of pricing practices.

Discounts should be removed when customers have become unprofitable or when the discounts are no longer deserved or valid. Effective communication can reduce the relationship risk when discounts are removed or when prices are increased. As a general rule, good communication should accompany any price increase that is not expected to occur without a notification to the customer.

Price increases can be accomplished as general overall price increases or as select price increases in response to cost or market changes. Most customers will accept moderate price increases in response to increased cost or as an annual adjustment to account for general inflation. However, customers generally don't like price increases due to supply shortages or added product features they didn't ask for.

The probability of successful price increases also depends on the magnitude of price increase. For customers with entrenched buyer inertia, most of the time, price increases of 2% or less are usually accepted without adding much risk to customer relationships, especially when customers understand the price increases are happening in response to cost increases or general inflation. Price increases of 5% or more are generally noticeable and higher risk. They should be avoided unless absolutely required due to cost or market price increases.

Keep in mind that every time you raise a price, you add risk to the customer relationship, and if you have already raised prices in recent history, another price increase may be significantly riskier, as you're now starting from a riskier starting point.

Price increases can also be less objectionable by focusing them on lower-risk products (non-image products whose margins may be relatively high and that have not had their prices increased in the last year or more).

Finally, since every pricing action should be a learning opportunity, the outcomes in terms of customer risk and churn should be hypothesized and measured, both before and after any price increase. And since the objective is to increase prices without creating additional risk or churn, the ideal approach will use "zero" impact as the hypothesis, and then plan and execute the price increase in a low-risk way, which should support the likelihood of proving the hypothesis true.

CHAPTER 19

# Pricing Strategies to Reduce Risk

*Risk comes from not knowing what you are doing.*

—Warren Buffet

## Chapter Overview

This chapter is about pricing strategies to reduce risk. The last of the five sacred pricing metrics is present value discount rate—a measure of risk. When there is more risk to the expected future profits, the present-value discount rate is higher, and those future profits are worth less. But as companies become more predictable in their ability to deliver consistent growth rates, investors will begin to value those future profits more, leading to lower discount rates.

Pricing strategies can affect risk based on the results they generate. There are three main ideas to keep in mind when constructing pricing strategies in order to manage or even optimize the level of risk:

1. Higher growth rates inherently increase risks.
2. Higher churn rates inherently increase risks.
3. Higher margins and higher prices inherently increase risks.

Growth is important, so lower growth rates to achieve lower risk is not an acceptable trade-off. But it might make sense to try to find ways to make growth rates more predictable, without constraining them in any way.

It's clear that reducing churn is generally desirable, and in doing so, overall risks to future revenues and profits are also reduced. So, any pricing strategy that reduces churn should also be good for reducing risk.

Raising prices and margins can have beneficial short-term results, but they can also add risk to customer relationships and increase future churn. Therefore, attempts to increase margins through price increases should happen only when additional risks can be sufficiently contained, and when it is certain that the new prices will not cause damage to existing customer relationships.

In accordance with Warren Buffet's quote above, one way to mitigate risk is to increase knowledge and information. **Therefore, any pricing strategy that results in the acquisition of new knowledge should be helpful to a company's efforts to reduce risk.**

As a general rule, there are three main ways pricing can reduce risk to present and future profits:

1. **Make growth rates more predictable:** The best way to achieve this is to increase visibility to the entire range of marketing-funnel metrics and conversion rates to better understand how pricing changes affect each metric. In almost all cases, Marketing and Pricing should be collaborating and sharing information about mitigation efforts if any metric gets "out of line."
2. **Reduce churn**: The natural way to reduce unwanted churn is to increase the strength of customer relationships. This is typically achieved by adhering to fair and transparent pricing and providing a good customer experience, which includes minimizing service failures. Pricing can help by ensuring fair pricing practices and by ensuring proper timing of pricing actions based on continuous visibility of customer satisfaction and unwanted service failures.
3. **Reduce variability of existing revenues and profits:** Pricing mechanisms like subscription pricing, long-term contracts, and vendor-managed inventory all have the ability to reduce the variability of existing revenues and profits, which in turn reduces overall future revenue risk. In addition, variability can be reduced by simply targeting customers that are more likely to be loyal, i.e., not shoppers and not opportunists.

Increasing available information is a way to universally reduce risk by enabling early warnings and mitigation actions. Anytime you include a customer touchpoint opportunity in a pricing strategy, you provide an opportunity to capture more knowledge and information, which can help reduce risks.

## Chapter Summary

All else equal, lower risk and variability are preferred because they usually translate to higher company valuations for the same amount of future expected revenues and profits. Risk is usually captured in the **present-value discount rate** (PVDR), the last of the five sacred metrics of pricing success. It's been demonstrated that a minor reduction in the discount rate can translate to an exceptionally large increase in company value. For this reason, risk and variability should not be ignored.

However, for growth-focused companies, reducing risk should not take priority over increasing growth rates if faster growth is possible. Reducing risk should almost always be a secondary priority. Yet there are some strategies that, by increasing predictability of results, can simultaneously aid in both accelerating growth and reducing risk.

There are three main ways to use pricing to reduce risk:

1. **Make growth rates more predictable**: Capturing early information on marketing-funnel and conversion rates allows for potential mitigating actions to achieve results that are more in line with targets, thereby reducing variability and maintaining desired growth.
2. **Reduce churn**: Improve customer relationships by fair and transparent pricing combined with good service and a good customer experience. Pricing strategies to incentivize customer loyalty can serve as another layer of protection to prevent customer churn and reduce variability in results.
3. **Reduce variability of existing revenues and profits:** Companies may also consider other risk-reducing commerce mechanisms like subscription pricing, long-term contracts, or even vendor managed inventory to reduce customer purchase variability. But in no case should companies let these mechanisms destroy their pricing integrity by devolving into customer-specific pricing. Any benefits achieved that way will not be worth the long-term damage to your customer relationships.

Lastly, risk reduction can also be achieved by avoiding disloyal customer types like **low-margin bottom feeders** or **opportunistic buyers**. To accomplish this, avoid any pricing strategies or incentives that would attract disloyal customers, and focus your incentives on dislodging the loyal customers of your competitors instead.

Pricing strategies focused on incentivizing customer participation in customer satisfaction surveys can help reduce churn and variability of profit results.

In summary, there are many ways to reduce risk, which can ultimately increase the valuation of future expected profits—the basis for total company valuation. While risk reduction should almost never take priority over growth, thoughtful strategy design can sometimes incorporate elements of both and allow companies to benefit from both higher growth and increased certainty of future profits.

PART 4

# Putting It All Together

*Without execution, 'vision' is just another word for hallucination.*

—Mark V. Hurd

CHAPTER 20

# The Complete Step-by-Step Process

*If you can't describe what you're doing as a process, you don't know what you're doing.*

—W. Edwards Deming

## Chapter Overview

This chapter outlines the entire step-by-step process for taking all the concepts, tools, and philosophies covered in the earlier chapters and creating pricing strategies that will have a massive impact to the value of your company. This process is depicted in the illustration below:

**Step-by-Step Process for Massively Impacting Company Value by Leveraging Focused Pricing Strategies**

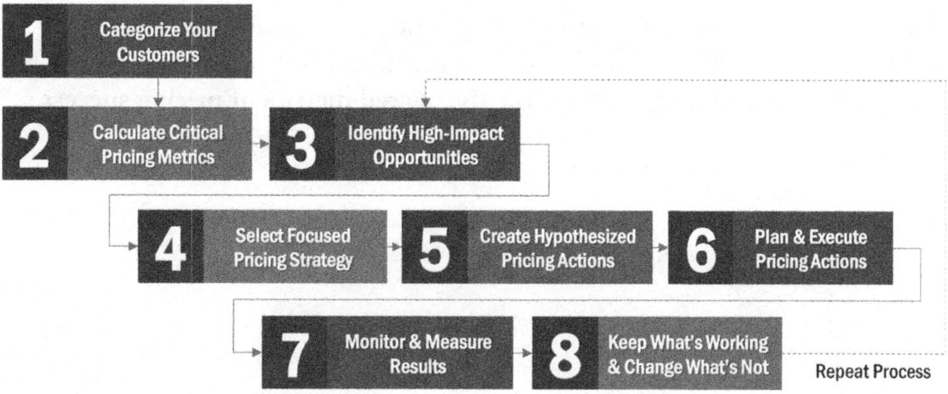

1. **Categorize your customers** to understand what type of customer they are and what stage in your customer lifecycle they occupy.
2. **Calculate critical pricing metrics** for each of your major business segments as a prerequisite to understanding the current state of the metrics and easy-to-see opportunities.
3. **Identify and prioritize high impact opportunities** based on their potential for increasing the value of your company.
4. **Select the most appropriate focused pricing strategy** to accomplish the desired improvement for the selected opportunity.
5. **Create hypothesized (or planned) pricing actions** along with break-even and hypothesized results, and then evaluate.
6. **Confirm, plan, and execute pricing actions** in order to set the strategy in motion.
7. **Measure and monitor results,** then validate or reject your hypothesis as soon as reasonably possible. Update your hypothesis based on what you've learned.
8. **Keep what's working and change what's not**.

*While an overview of this process is provided here, it is highly recommended that you spend some time reviewing the detail of this chapter in the full version of the book.*

You will soon see that this process can quickly produce an avalanche of value. You will want to ensure that you are communicating your strategy and expected results at all times, so others in the company can get aligned and not inadvertently sabotage the pricing results that are designed to have the biggest impact on the value of the company.

We will now do a brief review of each step.

## Step 1: Analyze and categorize your customers

Starting by determining the natural velocity of your business, you can then define or validate the definition of your customer lifecycle model, which will be the basis for measuring growth via the **five sacred metrics of pricing success**.

Analysis like the chart below will help you understand your natural business velocity:

**Number of Customers by Average Purchase Interval**

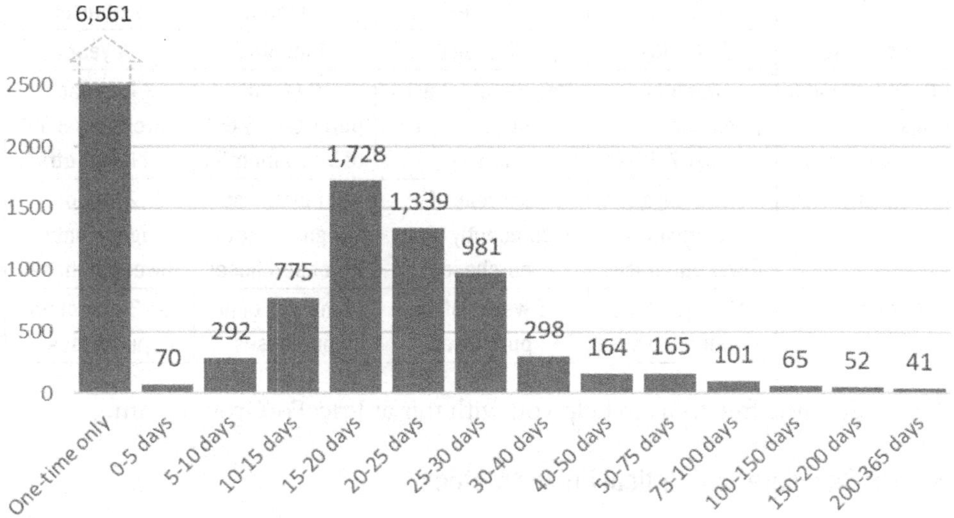


From this analysis, you can lay out the definition of your customer lifecycle model. The universal customer lifecycle model illustrated below can serve as a good starting point if you don't already have a defined model.

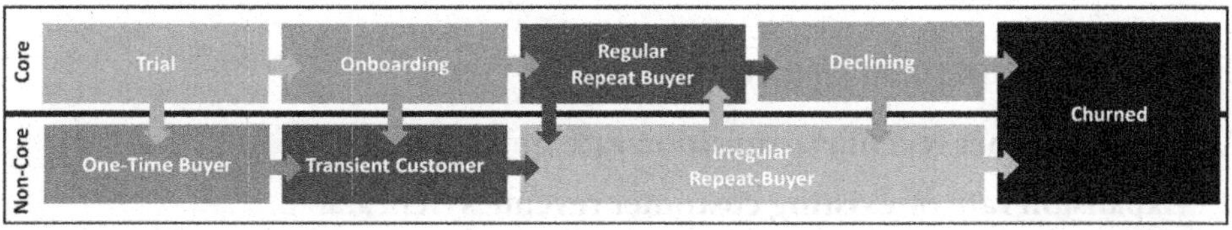

Then you can define the parameters of each stage. The table below provides a starting point for different business velocities.

| Stage | Business Velocity | | | |
|---|---|---|---|---|
| | Daily | Weekly | Monthly | Quarterly |
| Trial | 1–2 days | 1 week | 1 month | 1 quarter |
| Onboarding | 7–10 days | 4 weeks | 4 months | 1 year |
| Regular Repeat Customer | Regular purchases 5 out of last 7 days | Regular purchases 3 out of last 4 weeks | Regular purchases 3 out of last 4 months | Regular purchases 3 out of last 4 qtrs |
| Declining | 5–10 days of significantly lower purchases | 3 weeks of significantly lower purchases | 2 months of significantly lower purchases | 2 qtrs of significantly lower purchases |
| Churned | 10 days of no purchases | 5 weeks of no purchases | 4 months of no purchases | 2–3 qtrs of no purchases |

There are some free tools to help you with this at PriceForGrowth.com.

## Step 2: Calculate Your Critical Pricing Metrics

It's important to calculate your critical pricing metrics, starting with the five sacred metrics of pricing success, to understand and benchmark your current state and allow you to identify the high impact opportunities to improve your business. At a minimum, you will want to include the following critical pricing metrics:

### Five Sacred Metrics of Pricing Success

1. **New customer revenue acquisition rate** (repeatable)
2. **Expansion rate of existing customer revenues** (repeatable)
3. **Revenue churn rate** (repeatable)
4. **Annualized profits** (sustainable)
5. **Present-value discount rate** (a measure of risk)

### Customer Lifecycle Conversion Rate Metric

- **lead**-to-**trial** conversion rate
- **trial**-to-**onboarding** conversion rate
- **onboarding**-to-**regular-repeat-purchaser** conversion rate
- **regular**-to-**declining** conversion rate
- **declining**-to-**churned** conversion rate

## Step 3: Identify and Prioritize High-Impact Opportunities

After the critical pricing metrics have been calculated, you are now prepared to identify and prioritize the highest-impact opportunities to increase the value of your business. To accomplish this, you will evaluate opportunities across the **improvement opportunity hierarchy** illustrated below:

- Improve Value of Company via the Present Value of All Future Profits
    - Increase new customer revenue acquisition rate
        - increase lead-to-trial conversion rate
        - increase trial-to-onboarding conversion rate
        - increase onboarding-to-regular conversion rate
        - increase irregular-to-regular conversion rate
    - Increase existing customer revenue expansion rate
        - increase revenue per customer due to organic customer growth
        - increase revenue per customer due to wallet-share growth
    - Decrease customer revenue churn
        - decrease conversion rate from regular to declining
        - decrease conversion rate from declining to churned
    - Improve annualized profit percentage
        - decrease costs
        - increase net prices by removing discounts
        - increase net prices by raising prices
    - Improve present-value discount rate (reduce risk)
        - increase consistency of business
        - reduce business risk due to overly high prices

You will ultimately leverage opportunity tables that will direct you to the highest-impact, biggest-opportunity metrics to focus on, such as the summary table below:

**Improvement Opportunity/Impact Rank Table**

*This table shows the combined ranking of metrics based on which one has the biggest potential impact and the most room for improvement.*

| | Leverage Rank | Opportunity Rank | Combined Rank |
|---|---|---|---|
| Lead-to-Trial Conversion Rate | 1 | 1 | 1 |
| Trial-to-Onboard Conversion Rate | 2 | 2 | 2 |
| Churn Rate | 3 | 3 | 3 |
| Onboard-to-Regular Conversion Rate | 4 | 4 | 4 |

## Step 4: Select the Most Appropriate "Focused Strategy" to Accomplish the Desired Improvement

Once you've determined which metric you will focus on improving, you must consider the best or most appropriate method for accomplishing the improvement. I expect that, to answer this question, you will review the chapters that discuss potential strategies for your respective improvement metrics (Chapters 15–19).

For example, if you have chosen to improve your **lead-to-trial conversion rate**, what pricing strategy will you use to accomplish this? (Refer back to Chapter 15.)

- Will you offer a trial discount?
- Will you offer free services?
- Will you offer a rebate?

Once you've reviewed the potential strategies from the respective chapters, you can start putting together a strategy structure that you believe will be effective.

## Step 5: Create Hypothesized Pricing Actions

Once you've determined your chosen strategy, you will create a hypothesis of three values:

1. **Your hypothesized action**: the contemplated change in your pricing strategy
2. **The break-even outcome**: what is the minimum outcome that will make the investment positive ROI
3. **The hypothesized outcome**: what is your best guess of the outcome based on your knowledge and experience

## Step 6: Confirm, Plan, and Execute Pricing Actions

The next step is to confirm, plan, and execute pricing actions. While it sounds straightforward, this step should not be taken lightly. To be effective, some pricing actions require planning, education, enablement, communication, and time for people to adjust.

The plan must allow for the appropriate timing to ensure things happen not only in the right sequence, but with appropriate time for customers and other stakeholders to adapt. A well-thought-out plan will enable you to move more quickly, having already thought through different potential scenarios.

Executing means actually doing the work and making the changes—making sure that all the changes have been made in all the appropriate systems to ensure that advertisements, quotes, and invoices all have the correct pricing information. And they should all be instantiated (i.e., made effective) at the same time.

Don't forget that execution includes the entire plan, including adequate communication to ensure your strategy has a chance to be successful.

## Step 7: Measure and Monitor Results

Once you have executed a pricing action, you'll want to quickly verify whether or not your hypothesized outcome is being achieved. Although it may take several months to determine the entire impact of your pricing action, you will likely get much earlier signs indicating whether or not you are directionally in the ballpark of your hypothesized outcome, especially if you see results which are either significantly higher or significantly lower than you expected. You will always want to validate or reject your hypothesis as soon as you have sufficient data to do so.

You may also decide to update the hypothesis based on the learnings. That will allow you to accept or reject with more certainty and create better hypotheses for similar experiments in the future. For example, you may have an original hypothesis that conversion rates will improve by 50%. However, as the results come in, you may not have enough data to statistically confirm that 50% was achieved, as the limited data seems to point to 45%. You may decide to update the hypothesis to say conversion rates will improve by 35%, as that is more than sufficient to justify the move, and it allows you to immediately confirm the hypothesis of >35% as true. Now you can declare victory and move on to the next improvement opportunity.

## Step 8: Keep What's Working and Change What's Not—Document Your Decision and Move On

After you get to the point where you can either accept or reject your hypothesis with some reasonable level of certainty, it's time to move on to the next opportunity. Before moving on, you will decide to either stay the course and roll with the new changes or revert back and do something different.

At this point in the process, if the action proved to be beneficial, you would want to pause to reflect on the value you have just created for the company. You will want to document the before and after of both the key metric you sought to improve and the resultant impact on the overall value of the company.

Recognition is very important. But perhaps equally important are the collection of facts and the process of learning. When the facts change, it's an opportunity to learn.

At this point, you can return to Step 3 to revisit the new list of high-impact opportunities, so you can get started on the next area of potential impact.

## Chapter Summary

There is an easy, step-by-step process to use all the concepts, tools, and philosophies in this book to drive massive impact to the value of your company through focused pricing strategies.

1. **Categorize your customers** to understand what type of customers they are, along with their current stage in your customer lifecycle.
2. **Calculate your critical pricing metrics** for each of your major business segments as a prerequisite to understanding current state and easy-to-see opportunities.
3. **Identify and prioritize your high impact opportunities** based on the potential to have the largest impact to the value of your company.
4. **Select the most appropriate focused pricing strategy** to accomplish the desired improvement for the selected opportunity.
5. **Create hypothesized (or planned) pricing actions** along with break-even and hypothesized results, and then evaluate.
6. **Confirm, plan, and execute pricing actions**.
7. **Measure and monitor results, then update your hypothesis**; validate or reject your hypothesis as soon as reasonably possible; update your hypothesis based on learnings.
8. **Keep what's working and change what's not**.

This process will allow you to identify the highest-impact opportunities from your own data, ensuring that your pricing strategies will impact the value of your company more than you ever imagined.

CHAPTER 21

# TransformaCo's Step-By-Step Journey

**Case Parable 5: TransformaCo and Long-time CFO Bill Burley**

## Chapter Overview

This chapter is a case parable about TransformaCo, a $182-million manufacturer and distributor of exercise equipment and long-time CFO, Bill Burley, who for years had struggled to achieve the higher growth rates he was hired to accomplish. Using the principles of Price for Growth, he identifies high-impact opportunities using the five sacred metric and the tools discussed in the last chapter.

Five years earlier, Bill had implemented a major pricing strategy change by switching to exercise equipment subscriptions instead of one-time purchases, hoping this would spur a big increase in growth. But unfortunately, the expected growth never happened.

With the new book, tools, and concepts, Bill followed the process, starting with **step 1**, to determine his natural business velocity was monthly (monthly subscriptions). He then laid out the customer lifecycle model based on this monthly velocity. From this, he could move on to **step 2** and calculate his critical pricing metrics, which allowed him to see the areas of opportunity (**step 3**) most likely to make a big impact to the growth of company value.

Moving on to **step 4**, Bill realized that his biggest area for improvement was in the lead-to-trial conversion rate, where the company was performing significantly below their target benchmark of 33%, as shown in the Improvement Impact table below:

**TransformaCo Improvement Impact Table**

| Metric | Current<br>Min<br>Max | Typical Target | Standard Increment | Impact of 1 Increment on Growth or Churn | Impact of 1 Increment on Net Growth Rate | Impact of 1 Increment on Company Value |
|---|---|---|---|---|---|---|
| Lead-to-Trial Conversion Rate | 20%<br>0%<br>100% | 33% | 3.3% | 16.65% | 39.96% | 114% |
| Trial-to-Onboard Conversion Rate | 60%<br>0%<br>100% | 60% | 4% | 6.67% | 16% | 27.1% |
| Onboard-to-Regular Conversion Rate | 90%<br>0%<br>100% | 90% | 1% | 1.1% | 2.64% | 3.65% |
| Churn Rate | 16%<br>0%<br>100% | 10% | 1% | 10% | 10% | 15.38% |
| Margin Expansion Rate | 0%<br>0%<br>+2% | 2% | 0.2% | 0.25% | .01% | 0.13% |
| Annualized Profits | 8%<br>0%<br>+20% | 10% | 1% | n/a | n/a | 12.5% |

And so that is where he decided to focus. In order to improve this metric, he hypothesized (**step 5**) that removing the initial equipment set-up fees, combined with expanding the first month discount from 50% to a 100% rebate would lead to significantly more trials, and he constructed the following break-even table, which showed that this move would need to increase annual new customer sign ups by somewhere between 2% and 25% in order to break even.

| Break-Even Calculation | Incremental Cost (foregone profits) | Unitary Benefit (profit per incremental customer) | Break-Even Incremental Units (new customers) |
|---|---|---|---|
| Profit Break-Even | $3,650,000 | $1,440 | 2,535/yr (25% New Customer Growth) |
| ROI Break-Even | $3,650,000 | $9,000 | 406/yr (4% New Customer Growth) |
| | Valuation lost from profit decrease | Incremental company valuation per new incremental customer | Break-Even Incremental Units (new customers) |
| Valuation-Based Break-Even | $48,718,400 | $240,000 | 203/yr (2% New Customer Growth) |

They hypothesized that they could easily increase lead-to-trial conversions by enough to improve new customer sign-ups by at least 25%.

Moving on to **step 6**, they planned the new promotion and how they would market it to their customers, most of which would be accomplished by changing the ad content in ads they were already running. Within 90 days they were ready to execute, and they did so flawlessly.

After execution they followed **step 7** to monitor the results through key metrics. After a slow start the first two weeks, Bill was a little nervous that things wouldn't work as hypothesized, but then the numbers picked up. After 90 days, the conversion rates were averaging 25.4%, a 27% increase, which resulted in a new customer revenue acquisition rate of 30.48%. Offset against the churn rate which didn't change, the net repeatable revenue growth rate grew by 64.8% from 10% to 16.48%, which grew the theoretical company value by 375%, more than quadrupling the value of the company in less than one year.

Bill and his team, in their year-end strategy review meeting (**step 8**), decided to keep the new pricing strategy in place, as it had delivered results better than their expectations.

The next highest priority objective they wanted to attack was improvement in the 16% churn rate, so they went back to step two to recalculate their critical pricing metrics, and then to **step 3** to update their high-impact opportunity tables to confirm the priority.

In less than one year, Bill and his pricing team had found a way to break through the 10% revenue growth rates that had been constant for nearly five years. The company's stock price, which had not grown by more than 15% in any of the last 10 years, had finally grown by 90% in a single year. This was an important validation that investors preferred the higher growth rates over the foregone profitability.

## Chapter Summary

The TransformaCo case parable is an example of how one fictitious company went step-by-step through the process of segmenting their customers, calculating the critical pricing metrics, identifying and prioritizing high impact opportunities, and applying a focused pricing strategy to improve the value of the company. Obviously, the story was designed to show how a company can succeed in this process. But there are other lessons we can take away from this process as well.

**Focus on one major improvement opportunity at a time**: Sometimes, the opportunity impact tables will show two or more opportunities with similarly high potential impact. It's important to focus on only one major improvement metric at a time because it will help you concentrate your efforts and improve your chances of success. In addition, working on just one opportunity at a time allows you to better isolate cause-and-effect observations, so you can better understand what is driving the results you are seeing. Most of the time, the potential impact of just one opportunity is so large, there will be plenty of value generated by that improvement opportunity alone.

**Value trade-offs and break-even relationships:** In this story, increasing one metric (growth) led to the decrease of another important metric (profits). It's important to understand not just the profit break-even, but also the company-valuation-based break-even relationship. Typically, a company would not sacrifice 25% of their profits to grow revenues by 5%. But when you consider the compounding effects of the revenue growth by looking at the trade-offs in the company value calculator, it becomes clear that increasing growth can have a much larger effect on the value of the company than the reduction in annualized profits. In the TransformaCo story, they were essentially tripling the value of the incentive, and all they needed to do to make up for the profit loss, from a company-valuation-based break-even perspective, was to increase their net growth rate by 2%. This is often difficult to see without the five sacred metrics of pricing success and a company valuation calculator.

**Delayed results**: Sometimes, as was the case in this story, it can take a few weeks to see the results start to trickle in. They don't always manifest themselves until much later than you may initially expect. In this story it was a two-week delay before they saw any difference. Sometimes it can take months before customers start exhibiting the behavior changes you are looking to find. It's important to monitor results closely from the very first day, but don't assume it's not working if you don't see the change you're looking for within the first few weeks. If you don't see what you're looking for immediately, try to see if there are explainable reasons why it might take a little longer for the results to show up in the numbers. Sometimes it just requires a little patience.

While the specific details of the story can be entertaining, and even on the edge of realistic, the main lesson from this story is simply to illustrate the sequence of steps that should be taken to identify high-value opportunities and create focused pricing strategy changes to try to improve the objective metrics of those opportunities. Without the steps, it's easy to get lost or feel overwhelmed, but everything is manageable if you simply follow the steps, identify the break-even values of any potential strategy you are considering, and monitor the results after you execute any change, so you can know if it's working as you expected or required.

Using pricing to make big changes to the value of your company is very doable if you focus on the right metrics and follow the steps.

CHAPTER 22

# Moving Forward and Taking Action

*If you can't fly then run, if you can't run then walk, if you can't walk then crawl, but whatever you do, you have to keep moving forward.*

—Dr. Martin Luther King Jr.

## Chapter Overview

This last chapter talks about how to move forward and make real changes in your own organization.

Although it is a revolutionary approach, it is based on common sense principles and decades of experience. Most who have read the book and reviewed it agree with the fresh perspectives in this book because they make sense.

To summarize, these are the main concepts this book is based on.

- Sales-driven profit growth is more sustainable than price-increase-based profit growth.
- The value of a company is based on the present value of future profits.
- Maximizing the value of a company means maximizing the present value of future profits.
- Due to the compounding nature of growth vs. profit harvesting, increasing growth rates typically has a much larger effect on future profits than increasing prices.
- Higher growth and lower churn are achieved by creating stronger value propositions and relationships with your customers.

- Customers have a better experience when the price is fair, rational, and transparent.
- Contrary to popular belief, discretionary discounting does not improve the overall customer experience because it creates more work for the customer, and it leads to unfair prices.
- Different pricing strategies and actions will have different levels of impact on the value of your company, and you'll get more out of your pricing efforts if you focus on the highest impact opportunities first.
- Because growth rates have taken a back seat to margins in pricing and finance for so long, it's likely that strategies to improve net growth rates will be the highest impact focus areas for most companies.
- An open mind and a growth mindset will allow you make faster improvements to your pricing strategies.

But even though the principles are logical and make sense, most companies are not executing pricing strategies that align with this thinking. There are a few reasons, which I will share below, but keep in mind that the fact that relatively few companies are doing this means and opportunity for you to get ahead of your competitors by taking note.

Why aren't more companies taking advantage of growth-based pricing strategies.

1. **It is happening, but people don't see it**: Actually, many companies are pricing for growth. It's just not happening in very many Pricing departments. It's typically happening in Marketing or Sales.
2. **It's easier to mentally see the connection between pricing and higher margins than it is to see the connection between pricing and growth**: Finance and Pricing can credibly take credit for price-based profit increases, but they almost never get any credit for sales growth.
3. **Solutions are too focused on short-term impact**: Solution providers have gotten into the habit of justifying their value by measuring profit margin improvement, which is most quickly and easily obtained with a price increase.
4. **Seeing immediate results from raising prices is easier than seeing results from lowering them**: Lowering prices to grow volume often requires additional Sales and Marketing support, which involves unwanted complexity, while raising prices can often be done in a vacuum.
5. **Pricing for growth is not well understood**: Unfortunately, pricing and elasticity are complex concepts that most people don't understand very

well. Most fast-moving executives want simplicity and easy-to-understand solutions.

For the reasons listed above, Pricing must become the poster child for revenue growth. Anyone who has responsibility over Pricing needs to have "Growth" added to their title. VP of Pricing needs to become VP of Pricing and Growth. Pricing Analyst needs to become Pricing and Growth Analyst. Why? Because everyone else in the company needs to understand that Pricing is NOT the Growth Prevention department.

## The Five Sacred Metrics of Pricing Success Must Be Visible

In order for Pricing to drive the focused pricing strategies that translate to growth in company value, all relevant managers and teams need to understand the five sacred metrics of pricing success and how they contribute to the theoretical value of the company. The Sacred Pricing Metric Dashboard should be a key fixture in all meetings regarding pricing and/or growth strategy.

Prepare for resistance. Unfortunately, Pricing is a topic, where people like to weigh in as experts, even though they haven't put in the requisite study to really understand it. You are likely to run into some of these individuals as you attempt to lead your own company pricing transformation. For these people, it's best to stay focused on the overriding objectives and concentrate on common-sense principles. Potential controversy can arise when talking about the following concepts:

- Pricing should focus on growth rates more than margins.
- Pricing should be standardized and transparent.
- Discretionary pricing and discounts must be eliminated (this could be interpreted by others as a power grab by Pricing and a diminished role for Sales).
- Theoretical valuation of the company should be the single most important objective metric for all pricing strategy decisions (which is easily accomplished with the **company valuation calculator** based on **five sacred pricing metrics of pricing success**).

Best practices for proactively mitigating resistance include the following:

- Focus first on common objectives.
- Show the relevant data and highlight what the data means.
- Describe the change in terms of how each individual will benefit from the change.

- Indicate that, while change may be necessary, it doesn't all have to happen immediately, and you can work at a reasonable pace.
- Explain why others will benefit from the change and identify others who are already on board.

John Kotter, a world-renown expert in change management, is a great resource for information on managing change, as well as Prosci (www.prosci.com). I rely on both anytime I am undertaking a massive change project.

The following recommendations should help to prevent some of the difficulties that can accompany individual resistance to change:

- Focus on the self-interest of each stakeholder.
- Allow for different views of the situation.
- Try to communicate very clearly to avoid misunderstandings and miscommunication.
- Be empathetic to the negative effects and personal disruption that can come with change.

There are proven ways to overcome resistance and create lasting change that will bring enormous rewards to you and your company. Never let a little resistance get in the way of your success! There is too much value for you to unlock!

## You Will Succeed!

*Price for Growth* is not just a recipe for pricing success, it is a path to massively impact the value of your company. It is not out of the question for you to literally double the value of your company in less than a year just by focusing on the right pricing strategies and improvements.

With this new knowledge, you are now armed with game-changing concepts that will help you make a huge difference in your company. Your new playing field is now the value of the whole company—the present value of all future profits. You now understand why the strength of customer relationships will be more important than ever. With the five sacred metrics of pricing success, you now have a framework to measure what's most important and how it affects the value of the company. You have a significant advantage over your competitors who are still trying to balance growth and profitability, especially those who are prioritizing margin expansion over growth. These are battles your company will easily win. And you will lead the charge.

Your ability to succeed will become greater as you incorporate the **growth mindset**, which will keep you focused on learning and discovering the infinite possibilities to solve any of the challenges you may face. Your knowledge of the **80/20 principle** will keep you focused on the opportunities that have the largest impact, allowing you to produce even more extraordinary results.

## You're Not Alone

Believe it or not, if you are moved or inspired by the contents of this book, you are not alone. Please reach out if you'd ever like to bounce an idea off me or share an experience. I wish you the best, and I have faith you will make a difference in the world by finding ways to bring your ideas to life.

Good luck!

THE END

*Note: The full version of Price for Growth includes both a glossary and index, as well as 5 appendices with additional drill-down material. I highly recommend referring to the full version of this book to get more detail on any of the topics covered in this abbreviated summary.*

Made in the USA
Monee, IL
05 November 2026

67986827R00095